No Self, No Problem

No Self, No Problem

Awakening to Our True Nature

Anam Thubten

Edited by Sharon Roe

SHAMBHALA
Boston & London
2013

Shambhala Publications, Inc.
Horticultural Hall
300 Massachusetts Avenue
Boston, Massachusetts 02115
www.shambhala.com

9 8 7 6 5 4 3 2 1

Printed in the United States of America

⊗ This edition is printed on acid-free paper that meets the
American National Standards Institute z39.48 Standard.
♻ This book is printed on 30% postconsumer recycled paper.
For more information please visit www.shambhala.com.
Distributed in the United States by Random House, Inc., and in
Canada by Random House of Canada Ltd

Designed and typeset by Lora Zorian

LIBRARY OF CONGRESS CATALOGING-IN-PUBLICATION DATA

Thubten, Anam.
No self, no problem: awakening to our true nature / Anam Thubten;
edited by Sharon Roe.
pages   cm
ISBN 978-1-55939-404-8 (pbk.)
1. Religious life—Buddhism. I. Roe, Sharon (Sharon J.) II. Title.
BQ5410.T58 2013
294.3'4—dc23
2012048992

Sky is free.
Ocean is blissful.
Trees are divine.
Rocks are enlightened.
So are we.
Who is still searching...
for what?

—Anam Thubten

Contents

Contents

Editor's Preface

I MET ANAM THUBTEN shortly after he returned to the San Francisco Bay Area. At that time students were invited into his living room on Saturday mornings for a short meditation practice followed by a talk. The talks were always spectacular, startling, and devoted to the most essential truths based on Rinpoche's personal experience of walking the spiritual path. They cut through layers of speculation, dissecting and challenging every fixed thought, every belief held as sacred truth. Rinpoche's target is always the heart of the matter, which he clarifies in simple words accessible to Western thinkers who may not have any knowledge of, or commitment to, Buddhism. As the group of students grew, Rinpoche's living room became very crowded. Sometimes students even sat out on the porch. Through the generosity of many benefactors, a historic chapel in the charming town of Point Richmond, California, was purchased. This book, based on talks given in Berkeley and Point Richmond, California, reflects Rinpoche's profound knowledge and insight into the human condition. He speaks with clarity, humor, and ruthless honesty and shares his spiritual journey openly and honestly.

It has been an honor and a delight to work with and to present now to a wider audience the teachings of this authentic, simple, and devoted man who has dedicated his life to expressing in words and actions profound messages of authentic wisdom and compassion.

—Sharon Roe

No Self, No Problem

CHAPTER ONE

Pure Consciousness

Our True Identity

W E IDENTIFY with our body made out of flesh, bones, and other components and therefore we believe that we are material, substantial, and concrete. This understanding has become so embedded in our belief system that we rarely question it. The results of that are the inevitable conditions of old age, sickness, and death. We acquire these conditions simply out of believing that we are this physical body. We always pay a high price when we believe in false ideas. This perception is not just held individually; it is held dearly by the collective mind of society and has been for many generations. That is why it is so strongly entrenched in our psyche. Our normal, everyday perception of each other is governed by this false identity and then strengthened and enforced by the language we use.

At a very early age we are indoctrinated into this notion of self as the body. For example when we see a small child we say, "He is beautiful. I love his hair. She has the cutest eyes." Through thoughts and comments such as these we are planting the seeds of this mistaken identity. Of course there is nothing wrong with giving compliments.

It is much better than criticism. However, it is still a form of misconception. The truth is that, independent of any characteristics, a child is inherently beautiful the moment she is born. So we are all beautiful.

We are living in an age when people are disconnected from their true identity and this false perception is validated from every angle. Everyone is craving a perfect body and seeking it in others. For example, when you go to the grocery store you see magazines displaying pictures of men and women in a perfect and idealized youthful form. It is very difficult to resist these messages. They come from everywhere, all aspects of society, and they validate this sense of mistaken identity. They validate the sense that this body is who we really are. Given the tendency to establish a perfect idealized standard, many people suffer from pride, narcissism, arrogance, shame, guilt, and self-hatred because of their relationship with their body and their ability or inability to reflect this perfect standard.

Every morning when we wake up and look into the mirror there is a voice in our mind that is constantly judging us and others according to this standard. Have you ever noticed that? Our mind is always judging: "Oh, another wrinkle. She is too fat. He is strange looking. She is beautiful. He is handsome." These judgments not only create a stumbling block on our spiritual path, they also create clouds of negativity in our consciousness and keep us firmly chained in the prison of duality.

But there is no need to hold on to this. There is the possibility of transcending this identification with our body in each and every moment. It is only when we drop all of these judgments that we will recognize that everyone is divine in their uniqueness. Egoic mind is always comparing self with others because it believes itself to be a separate entity and it uses the body as the dividing line between self and others.

We are nonmaterial. We are insubstantial. We are not like a table that eventually breaks down. The very essence of who we are goes beyond the conditions of decay and impermanence. Yes, our body is impermanent but our true nature is not impermanent. Our true nature is deathless and divine, transcending all imperfections. Because of this we are all equal, we are all one. Nobody is better or worse than anybody else. When someone manifests their true nature, they live out of love, kindness, and joy. They inflict less pain on others. When we meditate, sooner or later we discover that this is not just abstract theory. This corresponds to the truth, to reality.

What is our true nature if it is not this body? There are many words we can use to describe what our true nature is. The simplest word in Buddhism for that is Buddha Nature. The definition of Buddha Nature is that we are already enlightened. We are perfect as we are. When we realize this, we are perfect. When we do not realize this, we are also perfect. Our true essence goes beyond birth and death. It can never get sick. It can never get old. It is beyond all conditions. It is like the sky. This is not a theory. This is the truth that can be realized only in the realm of enlightened consciousness. This consciousness is surprisingly accessible to each of us.

When that awakening happens, there is no longer any desire to become someone other than who we are. Every previous idea of who we are vanishes and along with it the pain, guilt, and pride associated with our body. In Buddhism this is called *no self.* This is the only true awakening. Everything else is a spiritual bypass. This awakening is what we should be aiming for from the very beginning of being on the path. It will rescue us from falling into unnecessary spiritual traps.

When we are openhearted and ready to drop our previous perceptions of self, then spiritual awakening can happen at any moment. There is a beautiful analogy. Imagine a dark cave that hasn't been illuminated for a million years. Then one day someone brings a candle

NO SELF, NO PROBLEM

into the cave. Instantaneously the darkness of a million years vanishes. Like that, when your true nature is realized there is no longer this "I" searching for anything else. The awakening has nothing to do with our background. It has nothing to do with whether we have been meditating for a long time or not. It has nothing to do with meeting impressive teachers or gurus. It is simply dependent on whether or not we are open to it.

This opening, this receptivity, is basically related to our ability to resist arming the ego with concepts and ideas. A true spiritual path transcends all concepts and belief systems. It is not about reinforcing the mind's illusion of self as an identity. It is not about being a Buddhist, a saint, or a better person. It is really about deconstructing all of our illusions without any mercy.

It is very important to look into our mind to see what we are looking for, what we are seeking. This is especially relevant when we are going to receive spiritual teachings. When a spiritual teacher impresses us, we might discover that our desire is completely antagonistic to authentic awakening. Perhaps our mind is looking for comfort, for validation, for a spiritual high, or a new set of beliefs. Sometimes our ego convinces us that we are realizing this sense of no fixed self but at the same time we are holding on to another concept like trying to be sacred or spiritual. Holding on to concepts such as "sacred" or "spiritual" while we are working toward transcending self-attachment is very subtle.

Perhaps this sounds like a lot of work, like an arduous insurmountable task. It isn't when we find the secret ingredient. That is to know that this "I" is a fictitious entity that is always ready to wither away the moment we stop sustaining it. We don't have to go to a holy place to experience this. All we have to do is simply sit and pay attention to our breath, allowing ourselves to let go of all of our fantasies and mental images. Then we can experience connecting to our inner world.

As we begin to rest and pay attention, we begin to see everything clearly. We see that the self has no basis or solidity. It is a complete mental fabrication. We also realize that everything we believe to be true about our life is nothing but stories, fabricated around false identifications. "I am an American. I am thirty years old. I am a teacher, a taxi driver, a lawyer . . . whatever." All of these ideas or identities are stories that have never really happened in the realm of our true nature. Watching the dissolution of these individual stories is not painful. It is not painful to see everything dissolving in front of us. It is not like watching our house burn down. That is very painful because we don't want to lose everything. Spiritual dissolution is not like that because what is being destroyed is nothing but this sense of false identities. They were never real in the first place.

Try this. Pay attention to your breath in silence. Look at your mind. Immediately we see that thoughts are popping up. Don't react to them. Just keep watching your mind. Notice that there is a gap between each thought. Notice that there is a space between the place where the last thought came to an end and the next one hasn't arrived yet. In this space there is no "I" or "me." That's it.

It might be hard to believe how simple it is to realize the truth. As a matter of fact the Tibetan lama Ju Mipham said that the only reason we don't realize the truth is because it is too simple. If we look around carefully there are hundreds, even thousands, of indications proving the notion that our concept of self is unreal. Look at the face of a newborn child or a flower blossoming beautifully in a garden. They are all pointing toward this mystical realization. We might want to apply this simple inquiry whenever problems arise. If we feel angry or disappointed, simply ask, "Who is the one being angry or disappointed?" In such inquiry, inner serenity can effortlessly manifest.

There are stories about people who have been struggling with life's problems for a very long time without resolution. Once they sat down in meditation and asked, "Who is struggling?" they realized that from the beginning there was never really any problem. In a true sense this is the only solution that helps us. Everything else is just a Band-Aid that gives us a false sense of liberation for a short while. How many times have we tried these temporary fixes and solutions? Are we exhausted yet? If everybody on the planet, including the politicians, businessmen, and religious leaders, started working toward this realization, then the world would immediately be a peaceful place. People would be much more generous and kinder toward each other.

When all the layers of false identity have been stripped off, there is no longer any version of that old self. What is left behind is pure consciousness. That is our original being. That is our true identity. Our true nature is indestructible. No matter whether we are sick or healthy, poor or wealthy, it always remains divine and perfect as it is. When we realize our true nature, our life is transformed in a way we could not have imagined before. We realize the very meaning of our life and it puts an end to all searching right there.

Many people are looking for the perfect life in the distant future while they're busy wasting each moment of their precious life fabricating mental and psychological problems. We should remember that each moment is a threshold to perfect awakening. Awakening to our true nature is the key to unlocking the door of the paradise that lies within each of us. Paradise is not some kind of enchanted land filled with flowers and music. It is not some kind of spiritual Disneyland. Paradise is our primordial pure consciousness, which is free of all limitations but embodies the infinity of the divine. I remember seeing a bumper sticker that said, "I believe in life before death." To me this means that we don't have to imagine a future paradise. Paradise can happen right here, right now, while we're in this human incarnation. The choice is ours.

CHAPTER TWO

Meditation

The Art of Resting

I T IS VERY GOOD to ask from time to time, "What am I searching for?" This is a very powerful question. We may be surprised and shocked when we figure out what we have been up to. Often we discover that we have been chasing illusions. Sometimes they are beautiful illusions like the illusion of enlightenment and spiritual transformation. Nevertheless, as long as we allow our mind to chase such illusions, there is no true liberation. There are spiritual highs but no true liberation. It is very easy to have spiritual highs. Sometimes they are very pleasant, like enjoying a nice glass of wine. When we get depressed, sometimes we like to drink wine or sometimes we get up at one or two o'clock in the morning and stuff ourselves with ice cream. Having spiritual highs is a bit like that. It's just an antidepression, anticonflict, antisadness technique because it doesn't really cut the root of suffering in the ultimate sense. So we have to make sure that what we are searching for is not just another beautiful illusion. There are a lot of illusions. Life is run by illusions, believe it or not.

One time Buddha said, "I am beyond coming and going." This was the most profound teaching that he ever gave. What he meant was that everything is an illusion. That is the truth whether our mind can digest that as truth or not. Even Buddha himself is an illusion. In the same way, when we look into our consciousness we see that our mind is always telling us all kinds of stories. Everything we believe to be reality is nothing more than stories. "I was born in 1950 or 1960. I went to such and such college. I married. I divorced. I had children. I did this and that. I met with a great teacher two years ago and I found the path to liberation." It's all a story, all an illusion, imagination, fiction. The truth is that nothing is happening. Therefore we have to make sure that this, the egoic mind, is not just chasing after illusions again.

You may have noticed that we have a tremendous sense of fear and resistance when we believe that we are losing something. We always lose in our lives. We lose our loved ones. We lose our jobs. Sometimes we lose love from other people and sometimes we lose our fantasies. We are constantly losing. Eventually we lose this body too. We lose this entire universe when we lose this body. This is called "death." Whether we can accept it or not, the truth is that sooner or later we are going to lose everything when we die without any choice. No matter how beautiful our illusions are, they are all illusions.

The beautiful illusion that is unfolding right now will soon be lost. There is not even one single illusion that we can hold on to forever. We are going to lose everything sooner or later. The sense that it will last is only our mind telling us stories. Illusions are unreal. Illusions are mental projections. They don't have any concrete or inherent reality. When we look, we see that the egoic mind is always perpetuating its tendency to search for illusions, all kinds of illusions. It has done this for many lifetimes.

True realization is knowing that everything is an illusion. Without having that realization there is no freedom. Therefore, the goal of the true spiritual path is bringing about that realization in our mind and then living each and every moment in that realization. The goal is not just having that realization periodically but living in that realization as a way of life; sleeping in that realization, eating in that realization, taking a shower in that realization and sometimes fighting in that realization too. That's okay too as long as everything is happening in the context of that realization. We do not always have a beautiful smile on our face and dance all of the time when we live in such true realization. We still have to engage in day-to-day reality.

Realization is the heart of inner awakening. Without that there is no freedom. There is no liberation. Even though we think that we are transforming and that we are getting somewhere, actually we are just having another spiritual high, another spiritual illusion. The truth is that no transformation happens without this realization. So the real question is how can we realize the truth? How can we realize that everything is nothing but illusions, especially when we feel that our suffering is very real? How can we realize that all of the negativities and unwanted conditions such as illness are simply illusions? It is also not always easy to realize that everything is an illusion when we are having a good time.

Sometimes after we meditate we have a glimpse of this truth that everything is an illusion. But when we get off of our cushion and begin to deal with everyday life it is very easy to lose that realization. Sometimes this egoic mind has a tendency to work very hard trying to get somewhere, trying to realize the truth right now. It sounds very good, especially since I have been saying that this realization is the source of freedom. The ego will tell us, "This is good, I'm going to go after spiritual realization. I am going to do everything I can in order to get that as a spiritual reward." The ego will tell us to search for more knowledge, more esoteric knowledge, more training, and more spiritual complexity. Ego will tell us that the more complicated the spiritual information is and the more difficult the techniques are, the more profound they are. Ego tells us that the harder it is, the better it is. The more nonsense, the more mumbo jumbo there is, the more sacred it is. And therefore our ego sometimes becomes a workaholic, trying to figure out various spiritual training methods and gathering all of this conceptual information. Then it thinks, "Oh, I am really getting somewhere now because I am paying my dues. I am working hard." But the truth is that it never works that way. Sometimes these spiritual complexities and disciplines can be a hindrance, blinding our consciousness from realizing what is already there.

The Indian mystic Kabir figured out these ego games a long time ago. He pointed out these perilous traps to those who were practicing various spiritual disciplines. He said in one of his poems, "The spiritual athlete often changes the color of his clothes while his mind remains gray and loveless."

So we might like to ask the question, "What is the perfect path to awakening?" Of course there is no "perfect way" or no "only way" to the path of awakening. I always like to remember the image of Buddha Shakyamuni sitting for six years. This led him to awakening. Therefore, sometimes the best thing that we can do is simply just rest and relax. Ego may tell us, "That's too simple. Spirituality cannot be simply relaxing. There must be something more than that." But actually, ultimately it's all about relaxing. Therefore many Buddhist masters define meditation as the art of resting or the art of relaxing.

When we relax completely we see that all of our thoughts start to dissipate. The egoic mind begins to dissolve automatically. The egoic mind is very powerful and if we try to get rid of it, it doesn't really work. But when we just sit and relax it dissolves without doing anything.

Somehow we have the idea that the ego is the troublemaker. Especially if we are Buddhist we may believe that the ego is the troublemaker. We have names for the ego like Mara, which means the cosmic devil. That is the worst name you can give to anybody and that is the name given to the ego. Because we have been criticizing and bashing the ego all of these years, we think that we have to fight against it, resist it, and transcend it. The truth is that the more we try to transcend the ego the stronger it becomes. It's just like when you tell somebody *not* to think about a monkey. They end up having to think about a monkey. Therefore, sometimes it's good to just let go of all of the effort of trying to conquer and get rid of the ego and just rest. It is so simple. Everybody knows how to rest.

This kind of message is not really a new message. It's a very old message, an age-old message. The message is that if we just rest in this natural state of consciousness, in this very present moment, then this awareness, the enlightened mind, often manifests spontaneously. Enlightenment happens unexpectedly, in the same way that we are often struck with wonder when we see whales jumping from the surface of the ocean. They take our breath away. Throughout the ages these kinds of experiences have often been experienced by meditators. This is frequently noted in the Buddhist tradition. The beauty of this is that it doesn't require any special methodology or any special training. It often happens when we are least expecting it. Inner rest is the sacred ground on which we meet the light of enlightenment. This knowledge is inherent in all of us. That fact is indicated by the beautiful Buddhist metaphor of a hopeless, exhausted traveler who has suddenly and unexpectedly found soothing shade beneath a beautiful tree in the middle of a vast desert. The tree and shade symbolize the Dharma, or the path to enlightenment. In that sense, the path to enlightenment is utterly simple, although it may not always be easy. So there are no true excuses for us not to be ready to experience this mind. Every excuse is totally invalid and simply an example of the ego's resistance. Actually, we all know how to awaken because we all know how to rest.

Meditation is about resting completely. Not just physically resting but resting completely. Complete rest includes letting go of all forms of mental effort. Mind is always busy doing something. Mind has a very huge job to do. It has to sustain the universe. It has to sustain existence, because if our mind collapses then there is no universe. Just like the Buddha says, "Nothing is real. There is no nirvana. There is no samsara. There is no suffering. There is no imprisonment." There is nothing there when mind stops maintaining this virtual reality. There is no universe. It's like riding a bicycle. When you ride a bicycle you have to constantly keep pedaling. If you pause and stop pedaling, the bicycle doesn't run on its own. It just falls over. In the same way, as long as we don't create this imaginary world, this imaginary reality, then it just collapses. Whatever you call it, samsara, reality or illusion, it collapses. It collapses because there is no one there working constantly to perpetuate it. Because of this, the mind feels that it has a big responsibility. It feels that it has to constantly construct and perpetuate this world of illusions. So to rest means to pause, to pause from working very hard, to pause from continuously constructing this world of illusions, the dualistic world, this world that is based on the separation between self and other, you and me, good and bad. When you completely take away the egoic mind, the creator of this illusory world, then realization is already there and truth is automatically realized. Therefore, the heart of Buddhist meditation practice is to relax and to rest.

We think that we know how to rest. However, when we meditate we discover that the mind has a tendency to work constantly, to constantly exert effort and to constantly attempt to gain control over reality. Mind is not completely peaceful and relaxed. We find different layers of mind's effort. This is quite amazing to notice when we sit. At first we think, "Oh, my mind is completely serene and peaceful." But if we keep paying attention to our consciousness we see that there is a very subtle effort. This is the mind exerting effort, trying to have control over reality. Maybe mind is seeking enlightenment. Maybe mind is trying to transcend the ego. Or we might think, "I don't like what I am experiencing right now. There is pain in my joints." Maybe mind is trying to . . . whatever . . . finish the meditation session. Mind is always making up stories. It's always writing this cosmic script. Therefore the idea of resting completely involves letting go of *all* of this. Let go of all thought. Let go of all of mind's effort and completely be in that natural state of your mind, the truth, the "what is," and then realization is already there.

Sometimes it is very beautiful to just sit. Buddhist training begins by practicing sitting meditation just like the Buddha Shakyamuni, who sat for many years, did. This is the package deal that comes along with being on the Buddhist path. Sooner or later we all have to dedicate an amount of time to sitting. I always encourage everybody to take some time from their everyday lives to just sit. We can sit for twenty minutes, for forty minutes, for one hour, or for a few hours. Sitting meditation involves keeping one's mouth shut from gossip, idle chatter, and prayer. Prayer can sometimes be just another mental noise or an expression of blind faith and rigid belief systems. Because prayer has often been used in dualistic, fundamentalist religious traditions it is easy for us to misuse it. But this does not mean we should not pray. True prayer is the surrender of all of our concepts, including the idea of a higher power that will either reject or accept the prayer.

Please do not think I'm suggesting that we should not pray. We can pray as much as we want. All I am saying is that it is important to find a time in everyday life for sitting in silence. It's important for us to have some time every day where we can put everything aside and maintain a special silence. It isn't just an absence of commotion. It has the power to lead us directly into a deep peace where we can see the way things really are.

One time I visited the famous Notre Dame Cathedral in Paris. I was totally struck by its grandeur and I felt compelled to offer a prayer. Since I am Buddhist I don't recite any Christian prayers, but it also seemed strange to recite Buddhist prayers in this sacred place. Very naturally I fell into silence and I felt great peace. Just like that, it's hard to go wrong with sitting meditation.

So the heart of Buddhist training is to practice meditation. What is meditation? It is simply the art of resting and relaxing. I always like to tell this story. The story is about a monkey who came to the place where Buddha was meditating in a perfect posture. Buddha was in deep silence without any movement so the monkey did not know whether he was alive or dead. Buddha was so relaxed that when the monkey tickled him he did not react. Finally the monkey began to imitate him. The monkey sat in this perfect posture with his crossed legs and his head bent down a little bit. He began to pay attention to his breath and soon he became enlightened on that very spot. This is a beautiful analogy. It is profound and it is also very simple. Basically the story is telling us that the very heart of enlightenment is not complicated. It is not effortful. It is too simple and that's why it is difficult sometimes to appreciate sitting meditation.

In my own life I have done lots of sitting meditation and I often have thought that sitting meditation was not enough because there were no fireworks. Nothing special was happening. Also when somebody asks us what we have been doing for the past few years, it is very embarrassing to say, "Oh, I was just sitting." It seems better to be able to talk about the things we have completed. It is nice to present a list of our accomplishments. It can be very embarrassing to tell somebody that we were just sitting. Just sitting for six months or just sitting for a year. It is embarrassing for the ego to report this as so-called spiritual achievement.

Once we discover an affinity for sitting meditation, I believe it means that we are very close to awakening. Try to develop an affinity with sitting meditation. Just sit every day. First there are going to be all kinds of reactions to sitting. Ego is going to try to convince us that just sitting is not good enough. Ego is going to create lots of resistance. Ego will tell us that we are too busy, that we don't have enough time. We may have difficulty getting up early in the morning. We may experience procrastination. Our ego may tell us, "Today I don't have time to meditate. Maybe tomorrow I will meditate. Maybe in a month I will meditate." The ego always creates resistance. It creates gross forms of resistance which are sometimes obvious to see. It also creates subtle forms of resistance which can be more challenging to notice. But they are all aimed at preventing us from developing a regular meditation practice. So in the beginning we may have to force ourselves to meditate. We can make a vow to meditate every day if we are really serious about awakening. If we are really serious about discovering true realization, then we have only one choice and that is to practice meditation every day as the number one priority in our lives. It is often good to make a commitment.

I sometimes give meditation cushions to people to support such a commitment. When they sit, the cushion reminds them that they have a commitment to sit every day for six months. Sometimes it is very good to make this kind of vow in the presence of a spiritual teacher or even in front of a sacred image such as Buddha Shakyamuni. We don't have to be anyone special or know anything special to practice sitting meditation. Meditation is simply the art of resting and relaxing. It is so simple that we sometimes feel that it cannot be the ultimate discipline. We feel that there must be more.

I am speaking about a deep rest, an inner rest, a rest in which we let go of all forms of mind's effort, including mind's effort to maintain this illusory self. I am speaking about a deep relaxation in which we are no longer trying to hold on to anything. When we look at a sacred image of Buddha we can make a vow that we are going to meditate every day from now on. We can vow that we are going to carry this awareness and this enlightened mind into each and every moment. We can carry it while we are meditating and also while we are going about the business of our everyday lives.

We can make a commitment and dedicate our lives and our hearts to complete and everlasting awakening. When we make that vow then we find that there is a strength in each of us that allows us to overcome all resistance, all of the strategies set by the ego to jeopardize our path to awakening. This inner strength helps us to overcome fear, insecurity, doubt, and distraction. It helps us overcome everything.

CHAPTER THREE

Inner Contentment

Giving Up Nothing but Attachment

H APPINESS IS something we all want even though we don't
admit that all of the time. It is the very reason we are on the spiritual path. It is also the reason we are pursuing relationships, careers,
and all kinds of accomplishments. All of our activities are motivated
by attempts to bring about the happiness we all desire. So, it is good
to admit that we all want happiness. Sometimes we tend to get a little
pretentious. We don't want to admit that we want happiness because
it sounds shallow or unsophisticated. Since we are spiritual seekers we
think that we should at least have the pretense of wanting awakening
or enlightenment more than happiness. But at the bottom of everything, happiness is what we all desire.

There is nothing wrong with wanting happiness, but we have to
define what true happiness really is. There are many distorted versions
of happiness, so defining what happiness is is a very important step. Happiness is not something we can achieve by accumulating things, or by
realizing our beautiful illusions. Contentment is not the state of having everything. Contentment is the inner state where attachment and

fear are completely absent. Contentment is a state of mind where ongoing obsessive desire, "I want this, I want that," has completely ceased. So actually, contentment is a state of emptiness rather than a state of having everything that we have been fantasizing about and longing for.

Let me give an analogy. If we want to create space in a room and we begin by bringing in a lot of things from outside the room, it will not work out. The room will become stuffed with junk. So how are we going to create space? We should begin by just getting rid of things. We simply get rid of all the junk. Get rid of all of the things that are not necessary. In the same way, to bring about contentment we need a consciousness that is like creating space. It's not about having more, accumulating more. Rather it is about letting go of this and that. When we let go of everything we see that the space we wanted to create is already there. In the same way, inner contentment is already there and that is true happiness. There is no enlightenment other than that.

The true spiritual path involves bringing about contentment through letting go of all attachment. That's why the very essence of Buddha's teaching is called nonattachment. Buddha even defined Dharma as the path of nonattachment. But there is a big difference between giving up everything and giving up the attachment to everything. I don't think that we have to go in the direction of even trying to give up everything. That's impossible anyway. We can't give up everything. There are many things that we can't give up. It's obvious we can't give up our basic necessities. We need a home, food, clothes, and so forth. When we look at it, eventually we realize that actually we can't give up anything and this is all right.

For example, when I travel I always try to take a small suitcase. I fumble through all of my belongings and try to bring very few things. I look through everything. My toothbrush? I really have to take that. Toothpaste? I need that. Eventually I realize that I can't leave anything behind. It seems that the process of giving things up is like the process of packing my suitcase. So you don't have to give up anything at all. As a matter of fact, this path is about returning everything, returning all of your pleasure and enjoyment as a source of nonattachment, which is very ironic. But if you have a mind that knows how to transcend attachment inwardly, then this makes sense. Otherwise this doesn't make sense.

There is a story about the great Indian king Indrabodhi. One day he went to Buddha and asked, "I want to find liberation. What should I do?" Buddha said, "You must immediately become a monk and renounce everything." Since Indrabodhi enjoyed the pleasures of good food, entertainment, and so forth, he was not ready to give everything up and become a monk. He asked Buddha to show him a path to liberation where he didn't have to give up anything. It is said that Buddha then taught him a path that let him become enlightened without giving up anything at all.

The heart of spiritual practice is letting go of everything inwardly. It requires a very special understanding because it can be tricky. You can have everything but you cannot get attached to anything. You can eat ice cream but you can't get attached to it. Who can do that? Strawberry ice cream, we eat it and we get attached to it. We want more. When we are attached, we crave more and it's not healthy because it could be the last time we ever have strawberry ice cream. When we are attached to something we feel that we *must* have more. We just can't function without having more of that strawberry ice cream. We remember how delicious it was and also sometimes we use it as a kind of antidepression device. So this can be very challenging. We can have everything. We don't have to give up anything and at the same time we can't get attached to anything.

We have to remember that nonattachment is the only path to the great liberation. There isn't any other way. But it is absolutely up to us how we are going to undertake that path. There is no particular way, no perfect way to nonattachment. There are many ways, hundreds of ways that we can undertake the path of nonattachment. Sometimes people

like monks and nuns give up everything. That is their way of renounc-
ing attachment. And sometimes we simply don't give up anything. Just
like King Indrabodhi, we keep everything we have been protecting,
our career, possessions, lifestyle, position, relationships, and projects.
We keep it all without giving up even one single thing. And still, if we
understand the very heart of Buddha's teaching, then we are practicing nonattachment by inwardly rather than outwardly letting go of our
obsession and our identification with everything.

Let me get to the heart of the matter. What would be the most
skillful and effective way for all of us to undertake the path of nonattachment, especially if we want the path of the middle way, not falling into any extremes of either indulgence or fanatical austerity? What
would be the perfect middle path of nonattachment in our everyday
life? I believe that it is necessary for us to give up certain things in our
life even physically and externally. This has nothing to do with practicing austerity. In the East people take monastic ordination to dedicate their lives to a path of contemplation and to learn how to drop
attachment. This kind of lifestyle is not recommended for everyone.
It is very challenging to become a monk or nun, especially for those of
us who are living in a modern world. At the same time it is very good
to renounce one thing. Renounce something that serves as a distraction and indulgence. Renounce something that is keeping us from facing reality, some reality that we have been trying to avoid. There is a
part of us that is very scared and cowardly. This part of us puts up great
resistance because it doesn't want to go though the final, ultimate test
of letting go of all attachment and becoming awakened. There is always
a final test waiting for us. And we have to go through it to become
fully awakened, fully enlightened. If we are able to face that ultimate
challenge, then we will awaken on the spot. If we allow ourselves to
go through the whole process without running away, without having second thoughts, and without hiding behind psychological masks
of resistance, then enlightenment can happen right now in a single

instant. This is not a theory. This is not simply a speculation. This happens and it has happened to many great, extraordinary enlightened masters throughout history.

In general, we are very attached to many things. Each of these attachments is a powerful obstacle. We have to become aware of them in the same way that illness has to be diagnosed in order for it to be treated. We may wonder why we have to let go of our attachments. Well, this is the only way to ultimate happiness. Of course, these ideas do not immediately make sense to our ego. Our ego defines happiness in terms of acquisition and accumulation. The biggest reason behind our attachments is this sense of a separated self. Because of it we have a deep-seated tendency to easily get attached to things as a means of defining ourselves. We get attached to ideas and concepts because they somehow define us.

On the spiritual path people sometimes get attached to all kinds of sacred and bizarre concepts to make sense out of their place in this giant mysterious universe. In the ordinary world we get attached to sensual pleasures and entertainment for various reasons, most obviously for psychological comfort and distraction. So we have to observe truthfully and honestly. We have to see what sort of habits or indulgences or attachments we are using as a way of running away from something. It can be quite shocking to discover what we have been using to avoid inner pain. Sometimes even very simple behaviors and activities in our lives can be used as a shield against what we don't want to face. Watching TV can be a great source of distraction. I am not saying that watching TV is bad, not at all. I'm sure that there are wonderful educational programs on TV. But often people use TV as a way of distracting themselves from facing their own reality, their own shadow, their own inner sorrow and loneliness.

If we have been watching TV for a long time we may find that it is very challenging to be without this distraction for even a day or two. That can be quite challenging, almost a crisis. We may find that we almost cannot face the boredom. It is very painful because we are no longer distracting our mind from facing whatever is there. My recommendation, as a method of bringing about the wisdom of nonattachment, is to carefully examine our lifestyle and habits. Go through all of our usual activities and we will find a lot of habitual behavior that we use as a way of shielding ourselves from facing ourselves. Once we are able to pinpoint a specific habit, then we have to be very serious, deadly serious. We have to practice refraining from that specific habit whether it is watching too much TV, reading too much, chatting too much, drinking alcohol too much, or smoking cigarettes. Just pick one thing that we are really holding on to, one personal habit that we really cling to as a kind of refuge, and try not to indulge in that habit. This is good to do even if we cannot give it up completely.

There are certain things that we cannot give up completely because life would not operate. For example making phone calls is so necessary in this twenty-first century that it is almost impossible to operate our lives without relying on the telephone. And that's why there is no need to completely give up the telephone. But at the same time, if we realize that one of our tendencies to distract our mind is to be on the phone constantly and to chat and to gossip, then it will be quite transformational and liberating to just reduce that habit and try not to use the phone as we have been doing in the past. And that can be a discipline, a perfect spiritual practice.

Spiritual practice is not always sitting on a meditation pillow. For example, one could say, "My guru told me that I should sit for twenty minutes every day and meditate. I am doing that. Once I get up from that cushion I can do whatever I want to do." This approach is not going to work. This is a form of cheating oneself. Our practice of nonattachment must be a big part of our life rather than a small segment. One of the problems we often encounter is our inability to integrate our spiritual practice with our everyday life. We can practice the path of nonattachment and still live in the real world, without becoming a monk or nun and going to a monastery or convent. In the East many of the enlightened masters were householders. A great Buddhist master, Tilopa, was a fisherman. No one knew that he was a great master until his famous disciple, Naropa, recognized his realization. There is a benefit in going to monasteries or to retreats for certain periods of time to find solitude and to reflect on important things in our life. Yet in the end we have to integrate spiritual practice with everyday life where awareness and mindfulness bless our activities and interactions in each and every moment. When we live with awareness, our delusions and suffering begin to wither away.

Actually in the beginning we may have to struggle. If we are getting onto the path of nonattachment in a serious way for the first time, there will be some struggle. There will be moments when we notice that we have failed time after time. Sometimes we feel that we have failed so much on this path of nonattachment that we think we should give it up completely. Actually failing is absolutely fine because we have already completely and utterly failed. Why are we afraid of failing again? We have failed so completely that we have lost the sense of who we are. We have lost our unity with our true nature. We have lost the realization of who we are and that is the greatest failure there is. Nothing else is really a tragedy or a real serious failure in comparison with the failure of losing our unity with our true nature. This has already happened to all of us from the very beginning and that is why it is impossible to really fail again. Any subsequent failure is just an idea. "Oh, I am losing my job. I failed. I didn't pass my test. I failed again. My relationship is falling apart. I failed again. My meditation is filled with turbulence. I failed. I wasn't able to live the life that I fantasized. I am not able to live according to my ideal standards. I failed." These are all concepts.

The true failure is that we have lost our unity with our true nature. Beyond that there is no failure. Everything else is simply a perception, an idea. Of course we can live in that illusion of failure forever and torment ourselves day after day. Sometimes our mind is the greatest challenge we face, more challenging than anything we face from the outside. Our mind can be very destructive, very dangerous. Our mind can be our greatest adversary, especially when our mind chooses to live in unenlightened perceptions of reality. We can eat a lot of food, we can live a beautiful life, but still we will not be content as long as we are living in unenlightened perceptions. So failure is just a perception, that's all. It is okay to fail and to fail continuously, time after time. In fact, every time we fail we should give ourselves a chocolate as a reward. We can reverse the idea of failure and reward. Why not? It's okay to fail because we have already failed from the very beginning.

There is a stage in meditation practice where strong attachment to hope and fear disappears completely. They are replaced by a sense of certainty in ourselves and also in the journey we are on. From that moment on, even when we encounter emergencies, moments of fear, terror, loneliness, or desperation, we will not completely lose our sense of inner serenity. Eventually, through cultivation of meditation, nonattachment, and mindfulness, our serenity is always going to be there as majestic as a mountain. A mountain is so majestic that it can maintain itself in the face of an earthquake, in the face of a storm, in the face of thunder and lightning. In the same way, we are going to be able to stabilize awareness that is like a mountain, regardless of all that is happening outside of our consciousness and within our consciousness. Our awareness will be stabilized and eventually we will no longer identify ourselves with conditions.

When we identify ourselves with conditions, we don't have a sense of everlasting happiness or inner contentment. Sometimes we feel that we are happy and in the next moment we feel that we are unhappy. Sometimes we realize that we are awakened and in the next moment we feel that we are not awakened. Sometimes we are as shiny as the beautiful weather and sometimes we are very gloomy, just like the weather. Our consciousness is fluctuating between sorrow and happiness, joy and depression, pain and pleasure. Our mind is always oscillating between two extremes.

There is another state, the state of equanimity. When our mind approaches the state of equanimity it tells us, "This is very boring. Get out of this place." And then we tend to jump into another extreme of emotion or feeling. But right now we are identifying with the conditions, conditions of happiness and suffering, conditions of separation and coming together. When we identify with conditions we are always subject to sorrow and confusion and there is no source of everlasting freedom at all.

The fundamental premise of all mystical teachings is that there is a divine nature in all of us. In Buddhism we call this Buddha Nature. When we no longer identify with external conditions we are in the realm of equanimity. We are one with our true nature, which is completely indestructible, perfect and sublime as it is, forever. Buddha Nature can never be injured by what is going on right now in our life. It can never be injured by conditions such as illness, being rejected, or dying. Nothing from the outside can injure Buddha Nature. Buddha Nature is like a diamond. A diamond symbolizes that which is precious, perfect, sublime, beautiful, and indestructible—especially indestructible. In the same way our true essence is indestructible. It can never be injured by anything. In every moment we are absolutely perfect because our true nature is indestructible. Our true nature cannot be conditioned by anything.

Our true essence is perfectly sublime and divine. It is the highest thing in this universe. It is the most sacred entity. The true nature that we all share is more sacred than anything else. So if we are able to simply identify with our true nature, our pure consciousness, then all of our suffering is gone. That's liberation. That's it. There is nothing more than that. That's it. Once we identify with our pure consciousness, that's enlightenment. That's liberation. That's moksha. There's nothing more than that. Then fulfillment is always there without needing anything from outside.

CHAPTER FOUR

Mindfulness

Dissolving Mistaken Beliefs in the Fire of Awareness

B UDDHA WAS ahead of his time. He lived in a time and culture dominated by mythology, superstition and a restricted world view. Yet he transcended all of these limitations. He transcended all illusions and proclaimed that the only way to attain freedom is through realizing the truth. But what is the truth? How do we define it? Is the truth a theory, a concept? Is the truth some kind of omnipotent presence? Actually, in the ultimate sense, the truth is neither of these.

Truth is not conceptual. We can never understand or realize it through concepts and ideas. Truth is not to be understood. Rather, it is meant to be experienced, tasted, like nectar. There is nothing to understand about nectar. One must taste it, drink it, and experience it. The truth is like that. It is to be experienced and realized, not speculated about. We can theorize endlessly about what the truth is. We can keep adding more and more information, adding layers and layers of ideas and concepts to the knowledge bank of our intellectual mind. But none of that is going to be of any help in our quest.

"How can I realize the truth?" This is the heart of the matter and this should be our number one priority, our aspiration and our very deep resolution. If there is any healthy obsession, it should be an obsession with realizing the truth. We all have obsessions. Everybody is walking around with obsessions in their mind. Some people are obsessed with making money and others are obsessed with enjoying sensual pleasures. Some people are obsessed with their physical appearance, so they spend lots of money trying to maintain the youthful look of their face and body. Some people are very obsessed with their health and some people are obsessed with spirituality. Unfortunately, some people are even obsessed with hatred. They want to take revenge and destroy others. They are obsessed with thoughts of hurting somebody else to satisfy the very negative state of their ego. This causes violence and war, and results in pain and suffering. Some people are very obsessed with ideas and concepts, with accumulating knowledge. Ultimately, these are all meaningless obsessions.

In Buddhist terminology, truth is called "emptiness" because truth is empty of all illusions. Do not mistake this emptiness for a nihilistic nothingness. Emptiness is the source of all things. Emptiness is the infinite realm of love and compassion. Emptiness is the divine fire that burns all concepts and the holy water that washes away all misery. Yet from the vantage point of ego, emptiness seems to be the darkness of the unknown, something that threatens the very foundation of our being. But if you simply surrender all of your resistance, you will find that emptiness, or the truth, is your best friend. This friend has never left you and will never abandon you in the future. Once you fall in love with the truth you will have a never-ending affair and all of your longing will be fulfilled. One of the trickiest things, something that often prevents us from realizing the truth, is the tempting offers and numerous methods for attaining the truth. Most of these are unnecessary, just a way to postpone the final meeting with the truth. For example, we don't need a telescope to see what is in the palm of our hand.

In the same way, the truth is always in front of us and there is no need to go anywhere to find it. However, many of us, in our search for the truth, get caught up in performing empty rituals and engaging in intellectual speculation. Sooner or later, we become exhausted with this search and then naturally glimpse the truth that we have been searching for, for eons and eons.

Through embracing and living the truth, we realize inner freedom, which is the only nirvana to be found. Liberation is the cessation of all mistaken beliefs. Mistaken beliefs become obsessions. Obsessions are ego's shameless effort and struggle to once again sustain its flimsy existence. Nirvana is not some kind of beautiful, celestial garden filled with peaches and mangos, a place where everybody is walking around with beautiful halos. It is not a place where everyone is in a constant state of bliss. It's not a place where, the moment we arrive, there are a thousand people welcoming us, waving banners and playing trumpets. That's not really the definition of nirvana or enlightenment. It's not a place, a destination we are going to travel to. It's not even a transcendent state of mind that we are going to achieve. It is not a beautiful, ecstatic, trancelike state of mind that we can cherish. That's not really nirvana. Rather, nirvana is a great cessation of the separation between us and the truth. It is the mere acknowledgment of what has been the case all along. It is like waking up from a nightmare. It's a great relief to discover that nothing has to be done.

Sometimes I like to think about truth in the image of an old and wrathful Buddhist master who grabs us, shakes us, and shouts, "Drop it now!" Truth can be wrathful. Eventually it destroys all of our illusions, no matter how much we cherish them. The closer we get to it, the clearer we see that we have to let all of them go, even the ones that have been with us for a very long time. Sometimes we feel that we must hold on because there is just too much at stake if we lose them. But we cannot transcend our illusions unless we go beyond all of our belief systems, many of which have been given to us by others. Many belief systems are dictated by our culture, our upbringing, and by all of the conditions we have been exposed to since we were born. Letting go of our inner conditioning is a little like giving up our baby teeth. It can be a bit scary or uncomfortable, but it is necessary to make room for our stronger, more permanent, adult teeth.

There is an illogical statement that says you have to realize the truth to realize the truth. Is there any preparation for this rendezvous with truth? There is no ready-made perfect answer to this, even though there are many answers available out there. If we spend too much time preparing, we might get lost in preparation and never leave our old world. On the other hand, without preparation nothing happens. Everybody has his or her own way of preparing. One of the important criteria for this is to find a spiritual teacher who can help us wake up. Here I am not referring to a spiritual teacher in the capacity of a guru like in some of the Eastern traditions. A spiritual teacher manifests in many different forms and life situations. When we are one hundred percent willing to be free, the universe will be our teacher. Life itself will be our guide. A famous Buddhist quote says, "When the student is ready, the teacher will appear." The way to measure if it is the right teacher is to look and see if the teacher is adding to the illusions we already carry. We don't need anybody giving us better illusions. The best teacher is the one who destroys all of our belief systems and leaves us with our natural integrity. The true teacher will point out who we truly are instead of who he or she is. If we are looking for security and isms or if we have found them already, then we can be certain that we are walking away from freedom with the wrong teacher.

I keep saying to everybody, "Please open your heart. Please open your mind." You may wonder why we have to open our hearts and minds so completely. An open mind is a challenge to the ego. The ego always wants to hold on and protect what it knows already. For the ego, the unknown is always a nightmare. Surrendering to the unknown is like walking in a jungle at night. In the process of opening our mind, we lose our tight grip on the conceptual foundation of our being, which is simply mistaken identity. This false identity is a conglomeration of concepts, impulses, memories, and fantasies. From that combination, we derive a sense of who we are and a sense of certainty about how to navigate in the world. When we open our mind, our illusion of self will shatter and much of our familiar reality will shatter along with it. In human history, cultivating an open mind has always been an arduous task. Just think how long it took for humanity to accept the fact that the world is not flat and the fact that the earth is far from being the center of the universe. On the other hand, all of our scientific accomplishments have been possible only because some people dared to be courageous; they dared to open their minds to new ways of thinking, new ways of being.

What does an open mind mean here, specifically, with regard to our quest for freedom, truth, and nirvana? Nirvana or whatever you want to call it means the complete deconstruction of all of our rigid mental patterns and habits as well the deconstruction of all of our limiting beliefs. This deconstruction creates a space for true inquiry. When we open our hearts and our minds completely, we are in a place where we can experience something new, a new truth, a new reality, a miracle that we haven't experienced in the past. We can see things differently and they present new, expanded opportunities, new horizons. Therefore an open mind is required. This is true not only in relationship to the truth but in relationship to everyday life as well.

For example, when I first came to the United States, I was very closed-minded and very closed-hearted about Western food. I was very afraid of two things: the tomato and the avocado. The tomato reminded me of a clot of blood and the avocado reminded me of some kind of very repulsive grease. I had pictures in my mind and stories about them simply because my mind and my heart were not open to them. I was trying to defend my old belief systems about taste and diet. I wasn't ready to open my heart to the tomato and the avocado.

There was no way. All of these negative thoughts kept coming into my mind. "Well the tomato may be delicious. Perhaps I should try it some time, but not today. Maybe tomorrow or in another few months I will be ready to taste the avocado, but definitely not now." Actually there was really no good reason not to try a tomato or an avocado, but my mind came up with one reason after another. "Maybe it isn't delicious. Maybe it's disgusting. It looks like blood, very yucky." This was enough to keep me from trying either the tomato or the avocado and so my heart wasn't open for a very long time. Then one day, accidentally, my mind and my heart were totally open to the tomato and the avocado and I tried them. They were quite good. Now I love avocados and tomatoes so much that I actually cannot imagine life without them. They are truly amazingly delicious. They have totally changed my life. Sometimes I feel like holding my palms together in praise to express my gratitude to the tomato and the avocado.

The truth is similar to that. We just don't open our heart and mind because we haven't experienced the benefit of that. Once we have experienced the truth, there isn't even an issue. There is no worry. The whole question of whether we are ready to open our heart and mind to the truth isn't even a concern. But if we haven't experienced it, then it becomes a concern. Of course, we must know how to open our heart completely, not just halfway but all the way. Sometimes we open our heart a little bit and then we close it again. We open it and we close it again. We open our heart until we are almost there and then we find ways to close it. Ego jeopardizes our entry into the great liberation because ego doesn't want to give up control. Ego doesn't want to dissolve. Ego doesn't want to die. Painful ego doesn't want to dissolve because it's always clinging to this transient fleeting world of misery and conflict.

When I say "this world" I'm not referring to the physical world. The physical world is a beautiful world. There is nothing wrong with it. When I refer to a world of suffering I am referring to our mental world. We spend a lot of time in that mental world. Believe it or not we spend nearly twenty-four hours a day, most of our life, in this mental world, the world of duality. This world of duality and separation is permeated with ongoing conflict, struggle, and anguish because the mental world is made up of negative emotions such as hatred, anger, judgment, and so forth.

So the truth, or nirvana, is none other than a state where all of our mistaken ideas, all of our erroneous concepts, all of our illusions are totally abandoned. That is nirvana. Nirvana is like the sky in the sense that it's already here. It's always here. Right now. Nirvana is like a sky that is completely covered by clouds. But even when we don't see it, the sky is always there. It is always present, eternally. The clouds are just temporary, fleeting phenomena. Eventually they will disappear and the sky, which has always been there, will clearly be seen. Our mistaken ideas and erroneous concepts are the inner veils obscuring us from realizing the truth. Once we know how to remove those inner obscurations, those veil-like coverings, then the truth is instantly realized. Right there, we suddenly see that nirvana has always been there. What we have been searching for on our long journey has been with us all the time. We find out that actually we never left home; the whole search turned out to be a futile but necessary part of finding what was already there.

Whether we believe it or not, we are always in the realm of the truth. That ultimate truth is all-pervading reality. Nirvana is the realm of expression of that supreme truth. Sounds good, doesn't it? It is always possible to realize this beautiful truth from this moment until we die and then after we die. If that is true, then why are we working so hard, exerting so much effort collecting all of this spiritual information, without seemingly getting anywhere? This is quite paradoxical isn't it? We are like a person standing in a freely flowing river yet feeling very, very thirsty. We are holding an empty cup, begging everyone we meet to give us some water. Does the person standing in the river have even one convincing reason why he or she should not drink from the river? There is no reason. The only reason is that the person is looking in the wrong direction. He or she has forgotten to look down. All we need to do is to look down a little bit and then we realize immediately that we are standing in a river with a never-ending supply of cool, fresh water.

In that sense the spiritual path is truly simple. It is simple because it is not about acquiring, accumulating, or achieving anything. It is all about giving up what we don't need. It's about giving up what isn't useful instead of acquiring things with the idea of going somewhere or achieving something. That was the old game. That game which we have been playing for a long time is like a vicious circle. It has no end. Sometimes the spiritual search itself prevents us from seeing the truth that is always one with us. We have to know when to stop the search. There are people who die while they are searching for the highest truth with philosophical formulas and esoteric techniques. For them spiritual practice becomes another egoic plot which simply maintains and feeds delusions. Amazing! Buddha, God, truth, the divine, the great mystery, whatever you have been searching for, is here right now.

In Buddhism, the sole purpose of meditation is to awaken to the eternal nirvana in the here and now. Meditation is the direct doorway that miraculously leads us there. So, that's all we need. In the end, even that will be transcended. There are two very important stages on the path of meditation. The first is intellectual understanding. It involves investigating and inquiring into the nature of suffering and reality, nirvana and samsara, and self and other. Through that analysis, we come to this one powerful understanding, that ultimately there is no samsara to be rejected. There is no misery to be transcended. There is not even a self to be liberated. Everything is just our own concepts and nothing more. My misery, my enemy, my life, they are all my concepts. That's it. But it is possible to have that insight and still be quite miserable. Perhaps this is very familiar to many of us who have been meditating.

The second stage is going beyond everything. That means continuously embracing this understanding in your experience, living it, feeling it in your gut, and integrating it with the totality of your life. The good and the bad, the successes and the failures, are all part of the same duality. They are only real if you become attached to them. They are all like stories in a dreamworld that only appears in the mind of the dreamer. During this stage we learn to maintain an enlightened mind in the face of all conditions. We maintain an inner wisdom that transcends all conditions. Through embracing and living the truth, we realize inner freedom that is the only nirvana to be found.

The method of transcending is maintaining what meditators call "awareness." In the Buddhist teachings we always use this word "awareness." But the miracle, the function of awareness, is that it actually burns down all of our silly concepts, each and every moment. If I visualized awareness in a form, perhaps I would visualize it as a powerful fire. Awareness is like a fire because it burns down all illusions right there on the spot. So the function of awareness is actually burning everything down. Having awareness and practicing awareness means we are always ready to transcend, to let go of all beliefs, all concepts, and all thoughts in each and every moment. It's as if we were assigned to practice awareness twenty-four hours a day, as if we were the hero of awareness, completely alert and undistracted in each and every moment.

Some Buddhist teachers say, "Don't wobble." It means don't lose awareness. I love that expression. Don't wobble. It means be still and sturdy and strong and disciplined in terms of maintaining that firelike awareness in each and every moment. Once awareness is achieved then awareness is self-sustained. We don't really have to squeeze our brain to make sure that we are maintaining awareness. Awareness maintains itself. That's why it becomes effortless.

Whenever we believe that we have a problem, whenever we believe that we are real, the mind is actually lying to us, and deceiving us with a mistaken belief. Ego is tricking us into believing in an unreal illusory entity. Therefore our practice should be the constant work of being aware and transcending and eradicating all of our concepts and limiting ideas.

We just get rid of all of our concepts, all of our painful concepts, whatever concepts we are having an affair with. We are always having an affair with concepts and there are plenty of them. Every concept has a story line. Think about it. "I am poor." That is a concept. "I am stupid." That is a concept. "I am a woman." That is a concept. "I am a man." That is a concept too. They are all concepts. "I don't have enough money, but if I had a million dollars, then I would be happy." That is a concept. They are all concepts. Get rid of them in a single moment without even taking the time to meditate, without taking the time to analyze them. Transcend all limiting concepts as soon as they arise. Let them go even before we have had time to meditate, before we have had time to peel the skin to examine what's inside, before we have seen whether they are real or not. The idea is to simply let go of them.

If we take this message into our heart and are openheartedly willing to live up to it each and every moment, then I believe that we will be liberated. We will be enlightened. We will be awake each and every moment if we take this message to the bottom of our heart and live up to it as the ultimate guideline of our life. The key is at our disposal. Now we have to open the door to the palace of great awakening.

CHAPTER FIVE

No Self, No Problem

Ultimate Awakening

~~~~~~~~~~~

T HERE ARE quite a few ideas about what it takes to realize
enlightenment. Some people say it takes a long time to awaken
and some people say it takes a very short time to awaken. Some people
say there are ten miles between us and enlightenment and some people
say there are a billion miles between us and enlightenment. Sometimes
it is hard to decide which one is the correct perspective.

What is liberation? What is awakening? Actually, if we are searching for awakening as a moral reward or as an idealized utopian realm,
then enlightenment is like chasing after a rainbow. We can chase a rainbow but we can never catch it. Perhaps one of the main hindrances
keeping us from having a direct experience of enlightenment is our
preconceived notion of what enlightenment is. So we have to give up
every idea we have of what enlightenment is. Sometimes that can be
a little bit uncomfortable, especially if we have very high hopes about
enlightenment. When we are asked to give up every idea we have about
enlightenment, we sometimes feel that we are losing everything, even
our beloved illusion, enlightenment. How merciless and coldhearted.

But the ultimate truth, or emptiness, is the destruction of all illusions and that includes the illusion of enlightenment.

When we meditate, when we sit and simply pay attention to our breath, we begin to see that there is an "I," a self, who is searching for enlightenment and liberation from suffering. But if we keep paying attention to our breath and body sensations, then eventually all of those ideas, concepts, and illusions begin to dissipate one after another and truth reveals itself. It's like watching a mountain that is covered by clouds. In the beginning we don't see the mountain because it is covered by heavy clouds. But if we keep watching, then, as the clouds dissolve, the mountain begins to emerge and eventually, when all of the clouds are gone, the mountain that was always there appears.

In the same way, when we pay attention to our breath, body sensations, and to the awareness that arises, then all the illusions, suffering, confusion, sorrow, and personal issues, all of this begins to dissipate. We see that all of these experiences are born of delusion. This is the sense of "I." "I am real. I am truly existent." Everything is gone except this "I," this sense of self. Then, when we continue meditating, the sense of self also goes away. When we just keep meditating, when we just remain in that present awareness and observe, then the self dissolves too. When the self dissolves there is just pure awareness. When the self completely collapses, there is this inexpressible, simple yet profound and ecstatic, compassionate awareness. Nobody is there. "I" is completely nonexistent in that place. There is no separation between samsara, bad circumstances, and nirvana, good circumstances, and there is nobody pursuing the path or chasing after enlightenment. In that moment we realize the essence of the Buddha's teaching.

I'll tell you a bit of my personal story. When I first went to the monastery I had many fantasies. I thought that it was going to be a journey full of visions, revelations, and angels with flowers descending upon me. Then one of the first prayers that we learned was called the *Heart Sutra*. The *Heart Sutra* can be very dry to those who haven't realized its true meaning. It is not like some of those beautiful, ecstatic, mystical verses. The line goes, "There's no nose. There's no mouth. There's no tongue. There's no sound, no smell, no taste, no touch." Anyway, we kept reciting the *Heart Sutra* every day until we had completely memorized it. More than memorizing it, we were able to recite it so fast it was unbelievable. Then one day many years after memorizing and reciting the *Heart Sutra*, I finally came close to a sense of affinity with the meaning of the *Heart Sutra* and the meaning of this notion that there is nothing there in the ultimate sense. There is not even the nothingness. This truth is the great emptiness. Having even a glimpse of that understanding can be very transformative for the rest of our life.

The very essence of all spiritual teaching is about dissolving attachment to the self, and about dissolving every attachment to form, sound, smell, taste, touch, good and bad ideas, and all concepts. It is about dropping all attachment without exception. In Buddhism we often say that one has to be a renunciant in order to bring about awakening or complete liberation in one lifetime. When we say "renunciant" we are not really speaking about becoming monks or nuns officially or externally but more about becoming monks or nuns internally. The ultimate way of becoming a renunciant is by giving up attachment internally, attachment to everything, not just attachment to samsara and the things that we don't like. We give up attachment to nirvana and the things that we love too, because when we are attached to nirvana that is just another way of lingering. It's another way of sustaining this flimsy ego. Therefore, we have to give up attachment to nirvana and to every form of ego because ego takes all kinds of forms. Sometimes ego can even take the form of spiritual phenomena.

Believe it or not, we often use the spiritual or religious path to construct ego identity, even when this is not conscious at the time. That is not a surprise, since the function of neurosis is to suppress awareness of reality. Fear, pride, exclusion, even bigotry, not only are they far from being dissolved, rather they're being well maintained. This is what we've been doing for thousands of years, since the dawn of civilization and it is still one of our favorite behaviors, not in any one particular circle, but in every religious tradition. This may continue indefinitely on a large scale, since we're still evolving. Buddha realized that we cannot be liberated as long as we are holding on to any form of neurosis. Before him, in Indian culture, neurotic patterns were able to leak into the sacred teachings and scriptures. Things such as the caste system and discrimination based on gender were considered normal. Buddha was the first to invite untouchables and women into his congregation, which caused lots of controversy and created opposition.

People always ask me what it means to be Buddhist. My reply is, "It means being nobody." The true spiritual path is not about becoming. It is about *not* becoming. When we let go of this futile effort to be or become somebody, freedom and enlightenment take care of themselves. We see that we are inherently divine already and we are enchanted to see how effortlessly liberation unfolds.

Ultimately we must dissolve all of the defense mechanisms of our ego. This includes the spiritual ones too, because sometimes ego manifests in different forms, in camouflage. Therefore, true liberation requires the complete renunciation and transcendence of our ego, the self. We might think, "This is the same old message, this idea about eradicating attachment to the self. I've heard it many times. More than that, I have failed at it many times. Actually I came here looking for a different solution. I still want enlightenment but I want a different method." Ego says, "I still want enlightenment but without this whole business about eradicating self-attachment. I will do anything except that. Please give me a break. Let's bargain a little."

Ego likes to bargain, to have an argument with the truth. "Ask me to do anything. I will jump off a cliff. I will restrain my sexual impulses. I will do anything. But don't ask me to do this. I can't do this because if I do I will die into the great unknowable truth." Once again, we start wiggling around this last assignment of dissolving the self or melting into what is. Actually there is no way to bargain with the truth, emptiness. Whatever we call it—truth, emptiness—dissolving into it is the only way. And the more we realize the truth, the more we realize that there isn't any other way.

The only way we can bring about perfect, total awakening, right now in this moment, is by dissolving the self on the spot. But there are two ways to do that: a painful and an ecstatic way of transcending. The ecstatic way is known as the path of bliss. The reason that we call it the path of bliss is because it involves an effortless way to go beyond the self. How do we dissolve the self blissfully? When we try to wage a war as a means of eradicating ego's empire we won't be very successful in the end.

As spiritual practitioners, especially as Buddhists, we have been declaring war on the ego and blaming it for all of our problems and confusions. Ego is our scapegoat. We blame everything on our ego as if it were a separate entity. We have a war with ego and sometimes we feel that we are winning the war and sometimes we feel that ego is winning the war. Sometimes the very self that is fighting ego is actually ego and that's even trickier. But sometimes we can just look directly into our consciousness and ask, "Who is fighting against ego?" Often everything collapses right there. Therefore, the path of bliss is really not about declaring war on the ego in order to get rid of anything we see as a stumbling block on the road to our imagined final destination. Rather it is about allowing the self to dissolve spontaneously by giving up nothing and going nowhere.

How do we do that? There are many, many ways. But in the end, it turns out that these many ways are ultimately the same. Sometimes we just rest and that is all that we need to do. In Buddhist teachings, meditation is defined as the art of resting. When we rest, we pay attention to our breath. We pay attention to our body sensations. At first we see a huge empire of concepts and ideas, but if we keep paying attention to that present awareness, that peace and serenity, then the empire of ego, that big castle of self-illusion, begins to disappear. In that moment, "I" is gone and what is revealed is pure awareness. It appears spontaneously, just like the mountain appeared when the clouds dissolved. Just like that, our true nature shows itself. In that place, there is no self and there is no other. We know this experientially, not conceptually. We know it directly and without any doubt. We know who we are. We know our true nature, right there, with complete confidence. It's extraordinary when we glimpse that.

Sometimes when we sit and pay attention to our breath, ego tries to jeopardize our path. Ego tells us, "Well this is too simple. You are getting nowhere. There is nothing special happening here. There are no fireworks. This is not going to lead anywhere." Ego is trying to seduce us into chasing some beautiful exotic illusion. But if we just surrender and remain in that present awareness, paying attention to our breath, then amazingly the self dies. There is no longer a self who says, "I don't like what is going on. I don't like this ordinary moment. I don't like just sitting here paying attention to breath." The "I" who doesn't like what is unfolding is completely gone and that is all that matters in the ultimate sense.

When self dissolves, everything is already awakened. Trees are awakened, rocks are awakened, birds are enlightened, and the clouds in the sky are enlightened. When the Buddha had this moment of complete realization, he discovered that this whole universe is already enlightened. More than that, he realized that every particle on the ground is enlightened. He saw that every particle is a Buddha paradise. In each particle there are billions and trillions of Buddha paradises. In each of those particles there are billions of buddhas residing. This whole universe becomes suddenly enlightened and perfect just as it is.

That does not mean that we are going to be completely lost in some kind of spiritual trance, losing our common sense, driving through red lights, wearing socks on our head, and so forth. Of course ego will tell us not to completely surrender our ordinary, self-grasping mind because there will be retribution. Ego is always trying to warn us not to be completely awake. A little bit awake is okay but not completely awake. Ego has many ways to convince us not to become totally awake. Sometimes it will give us treats by letting us get intoxicated by spiritual highs masquerading as true awakening. Other times it will strike us with terrors of doubt and despair, throwing us into a darkness that negates all aspiration.

The hindrances to inner awakening can be so subtle they are almost unperceivable, and usually they sneak through the back door. Many spiritual traditions teach us that we cannot be free in this lifetime. But even if they teach us that it is possible, they make it sound like it is some kind of a super attainment unlikely for us to reach. Some even go to the extreme of saying that it can only be achieved by surrendering to an outer authority. As long as we believe those rumors, we're not going anywhere but in circles. Our practice won't amount to anything more than a dog chasing his tail.

As meditators we can relate to those situations. When we have been practicing meditation for a long time, we know many moments when we have experienced extraordinary transformations and awakening inside. But part of us really doesn't want to completely renounce our attachment to suffering. We don't want to fully dissolve into that great truth, emptiness.

Part of us wants to hold on to that last attachment. We want to awake a little but not completely. It's convenient for ego not to awaken completely but this is the only way to liberation. Sooner or later we have to completely awaken. That means that we have to completely dissolve into that great emptiness, the ultimate truth of nothingness, without holding on to anything, not even enlightenment, not even confusion about liberation or truth. We have to let go of all of it. How do we do it? When we try to get rid of it, it doesn't work. It backfires because who is trying to get rid of it? There is nobody there in the ultimate sense. So this is about melting; this is about dissolving the self, and when we know how to dissolve the self, then liberation becomes effortless. It is like drinking nectar rather than working hard. In general, this is a way of dissolving the self ecstatically and without any struggle, without any resistance. Devotion plays a very important role.

When we pray, what we are doing is invoking the spirit of devotion. Devotion is about no longer resisting anything. We are no longer trying to hold the composure of this illusory entity, ego or self. Self is always collapsing and dissolving in each and every moment. It dissolves if we leave it as it is because it's not real from the very beginning. It's already unreal. It's already collapsing. When we try to construct and maintain the illusion of self, then we suffer quite a lot. We experience insecurity and madness because we are trying to uphold something that is already falling apart. Self is already falling apart. Suffering is already falling apart. And who is it that works so hard twenty-four hours a day trying to keep samsara together while complaining about it at the same time? Who is that person?

There is a bit of a dichotomy here. It's confusing too because we come to the spiritual path with a lot of enthusiasm and determination. We are complaining about samsara, our misery, and we are looking desperately for liberation. At the same time, we must remember that samsara is already falling apart. We may wonder how that can be. I have been stuck in it for many lifetimes. This vicious cycle is not falling apart on its own. The question is actually, "Who is the self? Who is the one who is trying to maintain that samsara?" Samsara is really very high maintenance. It costs lots of headaches and heartaches to maintain. Who is this self trying to construct samsara? Who is that person? Well, actually they don't exist.

A while ago I was giving a weekend meditation retreat and a middle-aged lady approached me during one of the breaks. "Are you asking us to die?" I answered, "Absolutely!" while joining my palms and bowing toward her in reverence. "You got the message, that's it. There is nothing more to learn." When I looked up, I saw her face lighting up in a beautiful smile. No doubt she knew the way to liberation at that moment. One has to allow this illusory self to die again and again.

This death is deeper than physical death. This death allows all of our anguish to dissolve forever. It is not the end of something. It is the beginning of a life where the flower of love and intelligence blossoms. One of my friends used to tell me that the only way that one can be a true spiritual teacher is to give up every idea that one is a teacher. He is absolutely right. You have to renounce the idea, "I am a Dharma teacher." He used to tell me that when we are able to completely transcend and cut through even that idea, then we can be great Dharma teachers. So what he was basically talking about is dissolving the attachment to any identification.

Imagine that we have a very strong belief in our identity or role in society. Imagine that you are a boss or a CEO. Imagine that you are considered a beautiful woman or that you believe you are a young person. Imagine that you are heavily identified with one of those illusions of who you are. See how much suffering and anxiety you can go through just trying to secure and maintain that identity. Many people want to be the boss, a leader in this conventional world. Many people want to be elected mayor or president because then that becomes their identity. And many people inflict much pain and suffering on other people in order to sustain that identity.

Throughout history leaders have sometimes served as amazing archetypes or models demonstrating how destructive and dangerous ego identity can be. Millions of people have lost their lives and suffered greatly because of people fighting over a position. What is a position? It is unreal. It's illusory. Attachment to any identity can be very violent and destructive. This is the very makeup of samsara. Therefore, the essence of all spiritual paths is about dissolving everything here and now without waiting. And again, how do we dissolve that self ecstatically? We are just present, paying attention to the breath, and then the self begins to dissolve. This sounds so simple.

We may think, "I have paid attention to my breath many times and never had any revelations." But that is the past talking, trying to trap us in that old pattern again. This time be aware and let go of that thought too. Sometimes we must pray. When our heart is completely taken over and seized by the force of devotion, then self does not have any power to maintain its composure. Ego just dies right there on the spot, without dismantling the self into tiny pieces and investigating whether they are real or not. There is no time for analytical meditation. There is no time to prepare to transcend the self. Self is gone the moment our heart is completely taken over by the spirit of devotion.

When we meditate I encourage all of us to have the attitude that we are meditating to dissolve the self. That's why we meditate. Hold this perspective in your awareness and let your dualistic mind dissolve for at least a half hour, or at least for ten minutes every day. When you allow yourself to witness that unexpected glimpse of the truth, where the self is dissolved, it's like drinking nectar. It's inexpressible. We often use the word "bliss" to describe that state. "Bliss" is a good word but it can be misunderstood. The bliss that I am speaking about has nothing to do with ordinary bliss. It's not like the bliss of having great food or other sensual pleasure. This is nonconceptual bliss that is not based on emotions but is based on awareness. We often say that realizing the true nature of who we are is like drinking the nectar of ultimate bliss. The more we drink, the more we are going to be addicted, which is very good.

It is not enough to drink that nectar once or twice. We have to learn how to drink the nectar of great bliss from the dissolution of self many times. It is not enough to simply remember having the experience some time ago. In the beginning we should drink this nectar of bliss at least three times every day. That's the assignment for everybody who is looking for liberation. Then as time goes by, we drink many times, hundreds of times every day. Eventually we drink a thousand times every day. After a while we drink in each and every moment, when we are asleep, when we are awake, when we are talking, when we are meditating, when we are playing music, when we are fighting with people. We drink that nectar of bliss all the time. This is called "complete total awakening" and this is our goal. This is our intention and our highest aspiration.

I remember a very short quote from a Buddhist teacher: "No self, no problem." It is really short but true and very effective too. There is always struggle in our lives either consciously or unconsciously. Many people in the world are going through struggles with social injustice, violence, and war. Even in the most prosperous countries, which are in some ways more fortunate because they enjoy many material comforts, people are suffering. Some people feel that they don't have enough money or that they are not beautiful or intelligent enough. They don't have an ideal relationship or they are worried because they are not enlightened. Many people suffer because of anger, hatred, and judgment. All these problems spring from the mistaken notion of what and who we are. This idea of "self," "me," and "mine" is the source of our inner struggle. It is like an author creating relentless agony in our consciousness.

When we go beyond the self then we go beyond everything. We go beyond every form of struggle that we encounter in life. For example, when I meditate, if I am not really ready to melt the self, then I am struggling. My ego is struggling. "Well, I want to be enlightened. I want to have that bliss that he is talking about right now. I want to feel good. I want to have rapture but it's not there. Time is running out. I want to transcend self but it is not working very well. That's why I am kind of frustrated. I am struggling."

So this kind of struggle is pervading almost every aspect of life. There are times when we are on the meditation cushion, where we are looking very holy, perfectly spiritual, and we are feeling blissed out. But sometimes we are so ordinary. We are talking on the phone shouting loudly. We are quite angry at someone. It is amazing how many roles we go through in everyday life. When we sit on the meditation cushion we are very holy. But when we are driving our car in traffic, talking on the phone, and somebody cuts in front of us, we become very reactionary. We may even start cursing. We don't look at all like the guy who was sitting peacefully in meditation a few hours ago. The idea is that there is always struggle. There is always struggle in different forms. There is struggle when we are meditating and there is struggle when we are not meditating, as long as the self is being perceived as real. When the self goes away, then we are already in paradise and there is nothing to do. There isn't anything to do and there isn't anything to acquire. So this should be our mantra for the rest of our life: *No self, no problem.* Keep this in mind: *No self, no problem.*

I know that in our deepest heart each of us has strong faith, real longing, and undying aspiration to go beyond the self. But at the same time there is a way that we also might allow ego to buy time. Ego is very afraid of its complete demise, so it tries all kinds of methods and strategies to buy time and postpone. If it cannot do anything else, at least it can always postpone. So it keeps postponing and postponing complete liberation. Therefore, we always have to be mindful about that and pray to remove all hindrances from our path. The hindrances on the path are actually ego's resistance to complete liberation. That is the ultimate hindrance. So we pray to go beyond all the hindrances and obstacles that ego casts on us, so that we can be awakened as soon as possible and so that everybody else can be awakened as soon as possible too. We must realize that the wisdom that lies within each of us can transcend all hindrances. That requires an act of empowering ourselves. Let yourself be a peaceful warrior. We are all born peaceful warriors. There is nothing to fight against outside. The peaceful warrior is the spiritual hero who conquers inner adversaries by the force of pure consciousness.

CHAPTER SIX

Acceptance
The Method of Effortlessness

E ACH OF US has a strong desire to live a life free from all unwanted conditions: illness, misfortune, old age, and death. A few weeks ago someone asked me to talk about old age. I could see from the expression on his face that he was experiencing fear regarding the problem of so-called old age. As long as we are living in this human form it is impossible to have a life that is completely free from the conditions that we don't want: old age, illness, and other kinds of problems. Sometimes we are so extremely fearful that we have what I call a phobia. Phobia is a psychological term that means we fear or dread something in an obsessive, even irrational, way.

This primal desire for perfect conditions is a complex mixture of our instinctual impulse for physical comfort and our unconscious drive to be free from anything that even remotely reminds us of our fragility and mortality. As a result each of us constantly fantasizes about having an utterly perfect existence. We want to be in a paradise, in a heaven free from every circumstance we don't want to face. In all of human history, no one has actualized that kind of a life. Still we maintain and feed this childish fantasy that if we fight hard enough against reality, then sooner or later we will achieve this idealized life, free from all unwanted conditions and situations. Some of us work very hard fighting against reality.

One time I was invited to a party. There were a few people drinking champagne and soaking in a hot tub and, while they were in these very nice circumstances, they were complaining about their lives. They were complaining at that same exact moment they were drinking champagne and soaking in a hot tub and right after they had finished eating a very nice dinner. You see that this is contradictory. In some sense this is a little out of balance. These people had everything. They were having a fantastic time in terms of enjoying worldly pleasures and at the same time they were creating an imaginary experience of suffering and conflict. What they were complaining about doesn't really exist. If you looked for a reason to suffer, you could not find it anywhere in the proximity of their current situation.

In the same way, when we think that we have conflicts and hindrances, most of the time we can never actually find out where these conflicts and hindrances are. That's because they are only found lingering in our consciousness. Our consciousness is like a factory where we create all kinds of imaginary problems. It is a big factory.

Many people are rightly afraid of pollution. They are afraid of things like air pollution from automobiles, factories, oil refineries, and so forth. But unawakened consciousness is, I think, much more polluting than any of these. It might be useful to visualize that there is a factory in our consciousness constantly producing the pollution of imaginary problems, imaginary conflicts. It is the full-time job of this egoic mind. No wonder most people are suffering.

People always suffer either consciously or unconsciously because they mistakenly believe that if they fight against reality then they will be able to achieve their fantasies. They will be able to achieve this childish fantasy that they can have a life free from all unwanted conditions such as old age, car accidents, not having enough money, being sick, having aches, and so forth. Maybe when we look back forty or fifty years from now, if we live long enough, the problems that we are struggling with today will be just a memory. Hopefully we will be quite awake at that time and we will say to each other, "I was so immature then. I really didn't have to take everything so seriously because everything is already emptiness." One day we will be able to say that.

In Buddhism it is often said that there are external and internal hindrances—in other words, external obstacles and internal obstacles. The external obstacles are the more physical obstacles that we all face—things like earthquakes, being tired, a toothache, a flat tire, or anything that gets in the way of what we want. Nobody is born under such auspicious or lucky stars that they don't have to face external obstacles. We are constantly facing external obstacles each and every day. The moment we wake up, our nose is clogged. That is an external obstacle. The toilet doesn't flush correctly. That is an external obstacle too. Our fingernail is too long and our nail clipper is missing. That is an external obstacle. These are small obstacles.

However, every now and then we can have a major life crisis, like discovering that we are terminally ill or that we don't have enough money to buy food. That happens too. That is happening here to some extent, but it is not as widespread as in parts of the world where, day after day, people don't have any food. Either there is none or they can't afford to buy it. People can't feed their children. They don't know if there will be anything at all to eat tonight. They have to go out on the street and beg. That's their only hope of getting something to eat. At least most of us know that we are going to eat tonight. External obstacles can be challenging especially when there is a life crisis like the death of a loved one. Also, we could become ill, unable to meet our physical needs. It is very difficult to be in that position when you don't have a sense of spiritual realization, when you are not somebody like Milarepa or Machik Labdron or even one of my teachers, Lama Tsur Lo.

Lama Tsur Lo suffered from a spinal deformity. He was completely bent over at the waist and could not stand up straight. He always used a walking stick. He couldn't walk without it. His physical appearance was the exact opposite of the Greek god of beauty, Adonis. The extent of his wealth added up to zero. But Lama Tsur Lo was truly content and very, very happy. He had great spiritual realization but he was very humble and wanted people to think of him as very ordinary, not as a special or holy person. When you have true realization, like the great masters, you can transcend everything. You can transcend illness. You can transcend every problem that you can imagine and even those that you cannot imagine. There's not one single crisis or life condition that you cannot transcend when you are completely liberated, transformed, awakened inside through the power of cultivating spiritual discipline. For ordinary people who don't have that internal liberation, the external obstacles can be very challenging, so challenging that sometimes it can actually push them away from the path to liberation.

There is a tendency in many of us to think that spiritual practice is going to fix all of our problems. We carry these unexamined, infantile hopes and fantasies. This has to do with the fact that our relationship with spirituality is often dominated by unconscious forces. It is not the squeaky clean business we hoped it to be. It is a tricky, painful, exhilarating, and ecstatic voyage. What could be more complex than that?

As long as we are building defense mechanisms, transformation will be exiled to the realm of improbability. And these defense mechanisms, wearing a spiritual mask now, comprise layers of denial, each one more subtle than the other. It is like finding a new cradle where we can be infantile again and have no responsibility for ourselves. Mommy and Daddy are projected onto an omnipotent god or guru who will take care of us eternally. There is nothing more gratifying than having no responsibilities. Conversion experiences are so sumptuous and juicy and vacation is so desirable. But this cradle is not well made. Sooner or later we will encounter its limitations.

When we become involved in a spiritual path, we see that it isn't going to fix all of our problems. As time goes by we begin to see that life's problems are not getting easier. There is no magic wand, so it is very common to lose that initial love that we had with our spiritual practice. Spirituality is not about fixing all of our problems and the earlier we find out about this, the less disappointment we are going to face. We have to let go of all of these fantasies. The earlier we let go of them the better it is. If we hang on to them, we often run into disappointment and that can sometimes create a huge obstacle to inner awakening. It can completely draw us away from the path. So we have to remember this and maintain the perspective that our spiritual path is not really a remedy or antidote that is going to fix all of our problems. It is not going to remove all of our unwanted conditions. We are not going to be loved by everybody because we are on a spiritual path. The world is still going to relate to us in the same way it used to. Nobody says, "Oh, now you are on the path. Now I am going to be much kinder to you. I'm going to send flowers. I'm going to create rainbows everywhere you go. I'm going to pave a nice royal road wherever you walk." On the contrary, sometimes it seems that the world becomes even more challenging when we are on the path because the spiritual path wakes us up. It requires losing all of our investment in illusion. Growth can be painful.

There is a saying, "Be careful what you wish for." We have to be careful what we wish for because sometimes if we pray for liberation, especially if we pray for liberation right now, then the world can be very wrathful and very challenging. When the world presents difficulties and obstacles to us it means that now, fortunately, we have the opportunity to pass through all of our reactions, all of our habits, all of our thought patterns, all of our karmic behaviors. We can rise above all of these illusory conditions and maintain the mind of the Buddha, blissful awareness.

Therefore, if we are determined to discover awakening at any cost, then we must also expect and be prepared for the fact that we may run into challenges and difficulties. These challenges are not always external obstacles; they are internal obstacles too. They include experiences of doubt, anger, irrational emotion, depression, and so forth. Even Buddha encountered a great challenge before his awakening. He had a vision that he was being attacked, ambushed by the forces of Mara, just before his total enlightenment. It was the defining moment where he had to choose between triumph and utter defeat.

So now the question is, How are we supposed to deal with outer conditions, the external aspects of everyday life? The answer is acceptance. We have to learn how to accept what is. This is the number one goal. Learning how to accept what is is the number one goal for spiritual seekers. Sometimes we do accept what is. As the great Tibetan saint Patrul Rinpoche said, "When your belly is full and the sun is shining upon you, you act like a holy person. But when negativities befall you, then you act very ordinary." This means that it is easy to accept the circumstances of our life when everything is going well. But as soon as our expectations are disappointed, in the blink of an eye we lose all of our saintly composure. When things are going in the opposite direction, it is very hard to accept what is. The spiritual precept, the discipline that we have to try to maintain in our heart in all situations, is learning how to stay open in each moment. When we are not ready to accept, we are completely under the jurisdiction of ego and we don't accept anything. We don't even like the fact that we are on this planet. But there is nothing that we can do.

Ego is the problem. Sometimes ego is very spoiled, like a child who is constantly throwing tantrums. Sometimes ego doesn't accept where we are. Sometimes ego doesn't accept who we are. Sometimes ego doesn't accept the way things are without any real complaint. So what do we do? There is nothing that we can do. Sometimes ego doesn't accept the fact that the sky is blue but there is nothing that we can do. You see. Sometimes ego doesn't accept that we are living on a planet that is permeated with natural disasters, earthquakes, floods, and other catastrophes. All we can do is accept that and learn how to surrender to the flow of all events.

When we accept the way things are we are able to love everything and everybody. When we are not able to accept even one thing in this world right now, then how could we ever develop boundless love? Lack of acceptance is conflict. Conflict is pain. It is psychological pain. It is a spiritual illness. As long as our hearts are tormented by that pain, we do not have the strength to give our heart to anything and because of that it is impossible to bring about inner awakening. Enlightenment, you see, is just another name for boundless love.

It is almost impossible to practice loving-kindness toward all living beings without addressing, in a meaningful way, the innumerable problems arising in our own lives. It is a contradiction, you see. It does not work. If our heart is tormented because we are not able to accept things the way they are, then it is impossible to open our heart. It is impossible to let go of all of our defenses and embrace others. Therefore we have to constantly practice and deepen our awareness. We have to remind ourselves to accept things as they are. This is pretty much what the teachings called Mind Training are all about. Mind Training in Buddhism is about carrying those perspectives and even reciting slogans, phrases like "I shall accept the way things are."

There is a wonderful student who writes a reminder to himself every morning when he wakes up. He tells me, "Today my practice is to accept the way things are." Or, "Today my practice is to love everybody." Today my aspiration is, "I'm not going to get angry. I'm not going to judge people. I'm going to be thankful for everything." He comes up with these amazing thoughts every day out of his utter devotion to spiritual practice. In the same way, we should turn our minds to reciting and carrying out those teachings, those enlightened perspectives, and say, "I am going to accept everything." When we accept everything then there isn't any problem. All problems dissolve right there.

When we don't accept even one small thing then a small problem can become a big problem. Just a tiny problem, when you don't accept it, can completely destroy your entire inner peace. Imagine that we look into the mirror today and suddenly realize, whatever . . . there is something wrong with our clothes. There is something wrong with our hairstyle. We have nice hair but then one hair goes astray. It is going *this* way and we want to keep pushing it, wanting it to go *that* way. If we take that seriously, it can be enough to destroy our whole day. At first it is no problem. Then we think, "I don't like the fact that one hair is going in that direction." Our mind has a tendency to blow everything out of proportion. "I really hate the fact that one hair is going in the wrong direction. I don't like it. I hate it." This dark thought keeps growing and before we know it our entire consciousness is taken over by that dark, poisonous thought. Then we become angry. We start yelling at people and they start yelling back at us. It creates this whole problem out of nothing. This might sound ridiculous, yet this is how most people live in the world. In general, we are dominated by our thoughts. We are not the master in our own house.

When we accept not just the small problems but also even the big ones, then they become very easy to handle. We become like those great, enlightened masters, who were able to maintain a mind of love and ecstasy even when they were facing death. There are many stories about the enlightened ones who died in great bliss and grace. They did not carry any unfinished issues. For them death is not a termination but a homecoming. Ultimately there is no one to die. But death looks very real when we are still identifying with small self.

As spiritual seekers we don't have to invite challenges but we do have to celebrate challenges when they visit us. I am not saying that we have to go around looking for trouble. That is not our assignment. But when troubles arise we must know how to surrender to them and accept them. We even have to be jubilant in a crisis and think, "Oh, this is such an extraordinary, golden opportunity to practice how to accept what I don't like. If I am able to accept this condition at this moment in my life, then I will be able to transcend all of my fear, all of my insecurities. This is a blessing in disguise." We have to almost prostrate to the challenges when they visit us without invitation. When they are actually knocking at our door, we have to be thankful to them. In that sense, as spiritual seekers, we have to take our whole life as our practice, as our path. Life is our path. From the moment we wake up in the morning until the time we go to sleep at night, our whole life is filled with opportunities for cultivating acceptance, patience, tolerance, forgiveness, awareness, and mindfulness.

We don't have to be in any special place to practice true spiritual discipline. We don't have to be in a temple or a place of meditation. Life is filled with many opportunities to learn and grow. A friend of mine died of cancer. He had an expression that he used when he was going through difficulties. He always used to say, "This is AFOG, another f‑‑‑ing opportunity to grow." That was his holy incantation, a little unconventional, but it worked for him. I remember him dancing and singing the last few months of his life. He told me that he had no fear. I sat with him while he was dying and he was totally peaceful. Looking at him was like looking at the face of a sleeping child. There was the same innocence and purity.

The internal obstacles, these are the more intimate issues. Imagine those psychological and spiritual issues that keep coming back. These internal issues keep coming back even after we feel we have resolved them. Sometimes we may feel that there is nothing left and then these obstacles that are almost like demons hiding in our unconsciousness come back. These are the demons of anger, demons of doubt, demons of loneliness, demons of boredom, and they always try to reclaim us every time we are on the verge of complete awakening. How do we deal with that? Ultimately we have to carry this perspective. We have to see that all of these demons are unreal.

Often we hear people talk about how they are stuck with their circumstances, their karma. They talk about how much they want to change the direction things are going. This is true especially when people keep running into one difficulty after another: divorce followed by job loss, illness followed by accidents, or when they are bombarded by emotional upheavals. The truth is that karma is not a set of misfortunes. Karma is a set of internal obstacles. It's made out of thought patterns and deep-seated habits. We are able to let go of this. Therefore our karma is unreal. Our karma is illusion.

Buddha taught that everything is emptiness. Problems of life, even though they appear unending and recurring, are emptiness and therefore karma is empty too. Karma is unreal. Karma is not a thing. It is not a substance that you can pinpoint, that you can break down, that you can build into a fire. Karma is internal. It is the state of your mind. It is the accumulation of your belief systems, your thoughts, your pains, and your anger. It goes back many lifetimes. Karma can be purified only by realizing the truth, the pure essence of who you are. Karma is not a substance like some kind of tumor in your brain or your heart that you can get rid of by performing surgery.

There is a story from ancient India about a Brahmin woman who was very devoted. According to her tradition she was supposed to bathe many times a day in order to purify karma and impurities. So she used to go to the riverbank every day to take a ritual bath in this holy water. One day an enlightened master walked by the riverbank and said to her, "You cannot purify your sins, your karma, by washing your body with water. If that were so, then all of the fishermen would already be enlightened." At that moment, struck by what that person said, she stopped and asked, "What is the true method of purification?" The master said, "The method of effortlessness." It is said that she became enlightened by following that master's advice.

True meditation is nothing but the art of abiding, without effort, where you don't try to get rid of anything. If you leave your mind as it is, you will see that nothing can bind you. In that awareness of nondoing your thoughts are like ripples and your basic consciousness is like the ocean. Karma is actually nothing more than thought. When you identify with thoughts, thoughts form karma. So whatever arises in your consciousness, bad thoughts, good thoughts, don't try to catch them. Watch them. It's like watching the waves on the surface of the ocean. They arise and they always go back. In the same way observe your mind without any effort. Remember that this is called the method of effortlessness. Don't try to alter or change the natural state of mind.

Sometimes we experience the arising of positive thoughts. "Oh, today is a beautiful day. I'm winning." Or, we think, "Oh, I'm wonderful, I'm good, I'm perfect." These are positive thoughts arising randomly. Enjoy them without identifying with them. Then sometimes we have the thought, "I'm really terrible. I'm the worst of the worst. Today is a terrible day. The whole world is against me." These are just thoughts too, negative thoughts. According to the path of effortlessness, don't attach to any of the positive thoughts and don't try to remove or transform the negative thoughts. Observe and watch them without being changed, just like you watch the waves rising and going back into the water. They all dissolve. Negativity dissolves and suffering dissolves if you can do that. This is also a more subtle form of acceptance. This is called the way of abiding. Remembering the above story tells us that through the method of effortlessness this devoted woman was completely awakened.

Imagine you are in the midst of your emerging problem and thousands of thoughts are racing through your head. You're alarmed, maybe even frightened. Somehow in this infinite universe there is this little you having a meltdown, just like a small insect being swept away on a leaf in the river. This is the situation we find ourselves in all too often. And yet all of this is just taking place in our head. Our thoughts are taking us for a ride without our permission. Basically, we're either seduced or overpowered by them. So, what to do? Surprisingly, we don't do anything. Just by watching and being in the present moment we find ourselves in a calm and peaceful space where nothing has ever happened. When we end up believing our thoughts and acting on them, then we're creating karma and we will be stuck with it. Usually when we believe our thoughts we tend to act on them. But by maintaining this nondoing awareness, all of our internal issues dating back lifetimes will vanish. How simple it is. It does not require any learning. So this is the secret to a free and joyous life. In the Buddhist tradition, this is the meditation that many monks and nuns practice all of their lives.

Have you noticed that many people place an image of Buddha in their homes and gardens? This has nothing to do with them being Buddhist or not. It has to do with the fact that this image invokes feelings of restfulness, of nondoing awareness, in the onlooker. There is nothing religious about it. It is a universal response.

One time a woman attended a weekend meditation retreat. I could tell that she was very enthusiastic. When I talked to her, she expressed her hope for purifying her karma and becoming enlightened. The retreat was about nondoing awareness. She asked me, "What is the next step?" I replied, "There is no next step. This is it." She was a little perplexed.

In general many spiritual seekers get trapped into adding all kinds of esoteric practice into the activities they are already engaged in. The only thing this will accomplish is to keep us busier than ever. We can completely miss the point. This is how ego operates to keep the karmic snowball rolling. There is an old saying that can apply here. It says, "There is no need to put a leg on a snake." It means don't try to make things complex. The path to enlightenment is simple and elegant. It is about deconstructing and transcending all belief systems and silly activities. Enlightenment is already taken care of. It would be much too big of a job to search for it. Let it come to us. In order for the sun to come in, the only thing required is to open the curtain or the window. Just like that, we open our heart and mind without chasing after elusive enlightenment.

CHAPTER SEVEN

Realizing Our True Nature

The Heart of Spiritual Practice

⟋⟋⟍

M ANY OF US are engaged in a never-ending search. Some of us are searching for God, some of us are searching for a guru, and some of us are searching for a soul mate. Fundamentally, this search is a long, nagging agony. Underneath it there is a sense of being separated from the universe or the divine, something fundamentally vital to us. If we look deeply into ourselves, we often find that there is a vacuum at our core. This leads to feelings of loneliness, despair, and confusion. In a futile attempt to fill this inner void we try to find meaning in our lives through attaining worldly goals and by distracting ourselves with entertainment. Some of these techniques work temporarily as a psychological Band-Aid. We get a bit of relief for a while but sooner or later our old misery is back. Nevertheless, we are tenacious in hoping that if we find just the right thing, then finally we will live happily ever after. While we are pursuing these futile dreams, all we are doing is *preparing* to live instead of living fully in each moment. We are preparing for an ideal life which we hope to realize sometime in the future. We are not living fully right now, here in each and every moment. Every moment of our life is wasted when it is run by this endless search. Our life is run by this preparation and it will continue until the moment we die unless we realize inner awakening.

There is no guarantee that we're going to live for even one more moment let alone another day. Today could be our last day. This breath could be our very last breath. So, it is time for us right now to live fully as if we had already achieved everything we are seeking. This does not seem very logical to our ego. Our ego argues that we haven't achieved the real meaning of our life and must keep searching. We are not allowed to live fully right now. We are all searching for the true meaning of life whether we consider ourselves spiritual people or just ordinary people.

The meaning of life is the main theme of most religious and philosophical teachings as well as the purpose of all of our human endeavors. Our deepest sorrows come from the feeling that we have failed to achieve this cosmic illusion. It is so painful that some people even engage in self-destructive behavior. Failure comes from the belief that we have failed in some way, not attaining our true purpose. We are not sure that we will ever attain complete satisfaction and this sense can permeate all of the corners of our life.

If nothing outside of us can bring true fulfillment, then where should we turn? This can be a very powerful and life-changing question. This is the same question that led Buddha to the path of great awakening. We might have to ask ourselves this question again and again until all of our possible answers have been considered and eliminated. Even some of what are regarded as spiritual answers should be eliminated as ineffective solutions, otherwise we could be clinging to more beautiful illusions. There are many beautiful illusions which are offered as a solution to our problem. If you look around, society is offering all kinds of beautiful, inviting answers. Magazines and TVs are filled with commercials that try to give us answers to the question about how we can resolve these feelings of inner emptiness. Also we are living and interacting with others who have completely bought in to conventional beliefs and value systems, and it is easy for us to fall into those traps too.

A true spiritual path is not about going against the world; it is about not getting lost in illusions offered by it. Its aim is to prevent us from letting ourselves get lost. We often get lost in our jobs, our relationships, and our ideas of accomplishment and perfection. People often look back at their life and say that at the time they were lost in this and that. We literally lose ourselves in situations all of the time. Sometimes we get lost in our jobs to the extent that we no longer know how to enjoy life. We suffer quite a bit because we hold on to dreams of unrealistic success, competing fiercely against each other, and worrying about the possibility of losing our job. Many of us are lost in these kinds of daydreams each and every day. Right now, if we look into our own life, we might discover that we are already lost somewhere. Or we might discover that we are into some kind of activity that causes a sense of great inner conflict. This sense of being lost is deeply connected with the fact that we don't know our true nature, who we really are. Of course we pretend we do know, while all the time we are clinging to all kinds of surrogate identifications. Ultimately, all of these problems stem from not knowing who we are.

Wanting to know who we are is a deep-seated desire in each of us. But usually we cling to the sense of self that we derive from identifying with our persona. Our persona is the role or roles that we play. Usually our role comprises many components, including our stories about the experiences that have taken place in our life: where we were born, our family situation, the schools we went to, the churches we associated with, our Social Security number, and so forth. But those are merely the roles we play. They are like masks we wear. We might call them virtual identities. We need those masks or virtual identities to function in this world. But when we believe that they are who we truly are, we suffer a lot when we think we are losing them. We are attached to them because we don't know who we are beyond these false identities. The prospect of losing them gives us a shiver. But sooner or later we lose them all. We lose many of these cherished masks even before we die. Every crisis presents another threat that they might be taken away from us. Of course we never want to admit that we don't know who we are, so we always pretend that we do. This pretense comes at a very high cost. The price we pay is that we cling to all kinds of false identifications and associations.

The skill we must learn is to use these virtual identities without becoming attached to them. We cannot throw these roles away as long as we live on this earth. There are people who try to live some kind of ideal life which is free from all conventional bondage, yet their approach sometimes becomes unreasonable or reactionary. Reacting to all of our social roles can itself become another role to hang on to. When we become attached to our roles they become a form of prison, and we feel that we must constantly sell ourselves in one way or another just to keep our life in one piece. This self-sacrifice doesn't bring what we are looking for. On the contrary, it causes a host of internal conflicts. It sometimes leads to depression, self-hatred, boredom, and despair.

Whenever we begin to inquire into the nature of who we really are, we are finally on the path to true freedom. Therefore all of the great Buddhist masters gave profound teachings on the art of meditation as the direct way to enlightenment, the realization of knowing who we are. To synthesize the purpose of meditation, it comes down to asking ourselves, "Who am I?" This question helps us undo all of the layers of our persona. It takes us to the place where we are no longer identified with them or the suffering which goes along with that. Then our persona becomes like a garment that we wear because it is useful. We wear clothes but we don't identify with them. We need a persona just like we need clothes. We don't run around naked outside on the street. People would think we were out of our mind. There is nothing wrong with wearing nice clothes as long as we aren't attached to them. Like all compounded things they are impermanent. They aren't going to last. If we get attached to the nice clothes, we can get freaked out if something happens to them. A tea spill on them can lead to uncontrollable emotions.

When we look into the makeup of our persona, we can see that it is not something that belongs to our true nature. It is something temporarily given by society that we are simply clinging to. But if we don't inquire into it, it seems that it is who we are. We are often under the impression that it is who we are and there is nothing more to discover. For example, we might run into someone on the street and start a conversation. The person might ask us who we are and what we do. We might tell them that we are a teacher or the mayor of the town. Every time we tell someone who we are, unless we have transcended all identities, we are reinforcing the falsehood of the image in our mind and we are asking the other person to believe in our false self. As time goes by, the false identity gets more solidified and more dominating, so awareness of the transcendental self doesn't occur at all since it is totally obscured. If we became of aware of it, we would all be spiritually awakened, spontaneously, right there in that very moment.

As human beings we are deeply insecure and we do not know who we truly are. Of course this problem does not show on the surface of our lives. We are always telling ourselves who we are, based on this notion that we are separate from everything else. This sense that "I am separate" is the ground of our sense of self. It is reinforced by various false identities that we cling to, notions that "I am this" or "I am that." Whatever beliefs we have about ourselves are just another extension. Most of the time when we look around, we immediately see that our surroundings are validating these false identities. For this very reason, it is a challenging endeavor to deconstruct this illusion of self. Every time we look into our mirror we might have some thought about ourselves. Each of these thoughts adds up. They become the conceptual bricks we use to keep building this illusory castle of self. Yet, there is a suspicion that this notion of self might be very fragile and transient, and this thought is silently lurking somewhere in our consciousness. Most of the time this suspicion is not brought into the light of awareness, but if it is, some deep, inner wisdom will arise without choice. Our suspicion of the fragility of this false notion of self can go in one of two directions. In general it becomes a source of fear, anxiety, and insecurity. We often see people who are fearful and overly defensive when it comes to their own identity. We ourselves tend to become fearful if our identity is threatened. But at other times the suspicion can go another way. When that happens, it can be a life-changing revelation that can lead us to the realization of the highest level of truth. This idea is not some new, lofty theory. It is timeless wisdom that has been realized by many people in human history. Buddha taught this wisdom, and in his tradition it is called *anatman,* or "no self." *Anatman,* or "no self," is the term used to mean that one has seen through this false sense of self. One has seen that this false sense of self is merely an identification with one's roles in life. It is just a mask, not the truth.

Inner fulfillment is lacking as long as we are grabbing onto this flimsy and fleeting "false identity" which we are so attached to. We are not in touch with our true nature. This false identity is merely an illusory sense of self. Yet there is a part of us which vigorously resists seeing this reality. Through true inquiry we directly see that this cherished self is just a mirage and is not a permanent platform to live and thrive on forever. Through true inquiry we can also see that what lies beyond this mirage is something that is amazingly beautiful and exalted. Once we realize this, we won't need anything ultimately. That is the end of all searches. When we realize this, we know how to live our life fully because nothing is lacking and all is perfect. This unconditional bliss is what everyone is searching for. Yet, many of us are pursuing it somewhere out there and sometime in the future.

Since the teaching of Buddha is truthful and inspiring, Buddhism has some of the richest knowledge on how to deconstruct the illusion of a separate self. Works by masters such as Nagarjuna and Shantideva illuminate and are a direct guidance to this profound insight. Today we might ask if some forms of Buddhism have shifted the emphasis away from this wisdom. It seems that things the Buddha himself was trying to get away from have somehow managed to sneak back in. This is an understandable situation. Remember ego is the trickiest master. It can always find a way to keep us enslaved in the realm of ignorance. Buddha's way is the way of inquiry. Truth can be discovered by inquiry. The ability to inquire is one of the most amazing gifts human beings have. When deep inquiry is not a regular part of our spiritual practice then we just get stuck with whatever trip we are on.

The inquiry I am speaking about has nothing to with the intellect or with acquiring more conceptual knowledge. It is not a way to acquisition. It is a way to eradication. It is the method of eradicating all concepts about who we are. This idea might be challenging to our usual way of thinking. Of course, this is totally expected. This is one of the reasons why we sometimes miss the main point of the spiritual path. Our egoic mind is not interested in letting go of anything. It just keeps picking up whatever seems appealing to it. But if we are able to get into deep inquiry, we will see that all of the concepts we have about who we are are fundamentally erroneous. They are forms of lies and they are told to us by others and also by ourselves. Most of the time, we hardly get an opportunity to question those lies. Even if we begin to question, we often stop before we finish the process because a part of us really doesn't want to die. This part is the old version of self. This old version of self is the sense of an "I" that believes that it is inextricably bound to conditions. For example, when we feel that "I am going to die, and it scares the daylights out of me," that is the old version of self. We know that it seems real to all of us. It seems as real as the sun and moon in the sky, as real as the coffee table in front of us. But remember that we once believed in many things that we no longer believe are real. When we were children Santa Claus was real to many of us. How could any-body dare tell a child that Santa is not real? But one day we figured it out all by ourselves. We simply knew that Santa was not real and that he had never been real.

When we realize that this old version of self is no longer real, then we are no longer bound to conditions. Death is no longer a terroriz-ing threat. We have literally transcended death. Our body might decay and collapse but that is not death to us. This deathlessness has noth-ing to do with the idea that our soul or mind keeps reincarnating again and again when we lose our body. Rather we know that our true nature is one with everything, so it goes beyond birth and death as well as beyond reincarnation. Does the sky die? Our true nature is one with the sky. Does truth decay? Our true nature is one with truth. Death is just another concept. When we let go of the concepts of life and death then there is no more death, and for the first time we are truly alive. But if we keep holding on to these concepts, then there is a death and life is a painful repetitious affair full of suffering. Understanding this, life becomes a mystery to be lived.

Our deathless true nature is who we truly are. It is only when we realize and live in accord with our true nature that life is completely fulfilled. Through this realization we can live fully in each moment and life is perfect just as it is right now. There is no need to fantasize about an idealized life in a future that may never come about. We all have a choice to live life fully. Every moment is a perfect moment to take that chance. Now is the time to wake up to our true nature. Why are we waiting and postponing?

CHAPTER EIGHT

Truth's Eternal Mantra

"Hey, It's Your Fantasy!"

W HAT IS spiritual realization? Realization means the enlightened mind or the wisdom that realizes the way things are, the
nature of reality. Only such realization brings about freedom. Realization is not some kind of exalted state of consciousness. It is not a meditative state of mind. Rather it is wisdom that realizes the way things
are, the nature of reality, the truth. Most of the time we are living in
an unenlightened state of mind and we never see the way things are.
We are often confused and lost in darkness, this inner darkness of not
finding our true nature. But the more we are able to be in harmony
with reality, the way things are, the less suffering and conflict we experience. In order to find true liberation within, we have to remove all
of our mental blinders and realize the great truth, the emptiness, the
openness, the fluidity of all things, all situations.

Most of the time our mind is in disagreement with reality whether
we accept this fact or not. We might all like to believe that we are in
alignment with a spiritual path because we are meditators. But we cannot be in agreement with the true spiritual path unless we are also in

agreement with the truth, with reality. It just doesn't work. Our ego wants to have the best of both worlds. Ego might want to be in agreement with the spiritual path as an idea but it doesn't want to be in agreement with reality. That's because the truth is sometimes rather painful to the egoic mind.

Sometimes we have the idea that we are in agreement with the spiritual path because we are paying our dues: "I am praying every day. I am meditating every day. What else do you want from me?" It's true our ego likes to think that we are spiritual seekers and lovers of the truth. Our ego likes to think that we have great love, faith, and unflinching devotion to the truth. But we have to accept this very bitter news, this very painful truth and that is this: there isn't any other way to be completely, wholly in agreement and in harmony with the true spiritual path unless we are also in agreement with reality. Therefore our assignment is to inquire into our consciousness every day to see whether our body, speech, and mind are really in alignment with the truth. That means that my actions, my speech, and my mind should always be in accordance with the principles of love, kindness, and compassion, which are expressions of the truth.

I am not saying that we have to be perfect. We are not perfect. We don't have to be infallible, free from mistakes. We can't be most of the time. We are always making mistakes so this is not about being perfect like some kind of saint or holy person. There is a prevailing tendency for people to choose a spiritual or moral ideal and try to emulate it. As a matter of fact, sometimes a whole religious tradition is based on worshipping an ideal and we have this idea that it is completely infallible. This can cause a split in our psyche which may lead to various negative consequences, such as hypocrisy, guilt, self-deception, and excessive forms of pretense, which ultimately lead to disappointment of self and others.

We have to accept shortcomings in ourselves and others and embrace them without demonizing them. We become free from them the moment we own them and recognize them for what they are. It is liberating to live according to the principles of a true spiritual path. It is very enriching. It makes us more intelligent and more openhearted. It makes us happy and kind. When we try to live in accordance with a cultural code or an outdated religious ethic, it is stifling and binding rather than liberating. We become more rigid, inflexible, and bound to all sorts of unnecessary and ignorant belief systems.

It is always powerful to inquire, to look into our consciousness and see whether we are really living a life that is in harmony with a true spiritual path. It's not just that we are meditating every day or praying feverishly every day. Are we truly living in harmony every moment or at least most of the day? We may find that we have been doing a very good job. If that is so, then we should treat ourselves kindly. Buy a nice whatever, as a reward. But if we realize that in the last few weeks we have failed, then it's good to pray. Prayer is very beautiful. I learned in my own spiritual practice that prayer is one of the most powerful forces to bring about transformation of consciousness.

Prayer is powerful and heart opening especially when we make a true prayer. True prayer is prayer in which all of our resistance is transcended. Sometimes it is very powerful to pray to the truth and ask, "May I overcome this delusion. May I transcend this delusion." When we make such prayers, most of the time we almost immediately experience this pure, brilliant awakened mind that is already free from all mental confusion and emotional upset. It's like we have climbed to the top of a high mountain and can see very clearly. We see the nature of truth as well as the nature of illusion. Therefore I recommend that we all pray. Pray to the highest entity. That is the truth. Pray to the highest truth to liberate us here and now. If we pray from the bottom of our hearts, then the inner realization always happens. The realization that I was speaking about earlier always happens miraculously.

As spiritual seekers we are sometimes sidetracked a little bit by learning all of these techniques, all of these meditative methods. At the same time we forget to pay attention to this very vital aspect of spiritual practice, which is to be genuine and to be simple and innocent. We have to be innocent in order to know how to pray. If our mind is completely loaded with knowledge, ideas, concepts, and pride, then often we do not know how to pray. But we know how to pray when our mind is completely innocent, pure, and not loaded with concepts and ideas. Sometimes we offer true prayer when we don't have any more ideas, any more solutions, when we are at the end of our rope.

I remember the time I was trekking from Tibet to Nepal with a few other people. It was very dangerous and there was only a little bit of moonlight. It wasn't very bright and we didn't have flashlights. At one point, we had to cross a fast-moving, thunderous, cascading river full of icy water. There was no bridge. There was just one log that we had to walk on to cross the river. I was terrified. In that moment I prayed out of pure fear. In that moment of total fear I had forgotten all of my meditative techniques. All of my fancy visualizations were gone, as well as all of my ways of analyzing mental states. Everything was gone. I was so terrified I couldn't remember anything. But when I prayed I felt this sudden bliss, calmness, and courage. I walked perfectly across the log and I don't know how I did it. This has nothing to do with a miracle of divine intervention. This is simply about letting go of all delusions, all concepts, all fears and just trusting in what is. What is is always perfect. We either die or we live. We are either poor or we are rich. We are either loved or hated by others. No matter, we are always perfect in what is. We are always perfect in that dimension of actually purified reality.

There is true prayer and there is pseudoprayer. Praying to a god outside of ourselves as an all-powerful father giving rewards and punishment is not true prayer. This kind of prayer has been done through the millennia by humankind. With these kinds of prayers on their lips, armies march against each other, each one believing their god to be the only true one. This kind of prayer can never lead us to the truth. It keeps us circling in a realm of fantasy. It is a fantasy, a fairy tale for grown-ups. True prayer wakes us up from the world of fantasy and brings us in touch with truth in the highest spiritual union, what we call enlightenment. This union is total integration with reality, not some mystical la-la land.

We can pray whenever we feel hindered by confusion, fear, or loneliness. We can pray even when we don't experience those gross levels of negative emotion. We can pray when we come across stagnation in our spiritual practice or when our meditation is not going anywhere. It's not a major crisis but our spiritual practice is no longer moving forward. At those times it is very powerful to pray. We can pray until our hearts are completely melted and all of our defensiveness falls apart. We can pray until we discover that we are completely in love with the truth, which was never separate from us in the first place.

Let me emphasize fantasy versus reality and what the makeup of fantasy is. Fantasy is of course a perception. It is always opposed to the nature of reality, or the truth. Of course we understand the usual meaning of the word "fantasy." People say to each other, "Oh, that's just a fantasy. That's your fantasy." But when we meditate we realize that fantasy is not just a small segment of our unenlightened consciousness. Fantasy is huge. Everything is pretty much a fantasy. When we meditate we realize that everything is a fantasy. The past is a fantasy. The future is a fantasy. Even the present is a fantasy.

When we anticipate the future, we sometimes start fantasizing about illness, death, and misfortune. This can completely destroy our inner peace if we get caught up in it. This seems to be a universal problem. Just think about this phenomenon of worrying. It is a mental disease that causes us a great deal of agony. This fantasy is not just an innocent case of daydreaming. It is a far more destructive force than we may have initially estimated and we never even question whether it is real or not. Buddha said, "With thought we create our world." In the same way we might say, "With fantasy, we create our world."

Some fantasies are quite easy to detect. The ideas that we are going to live forever, be young forever, receive an amazing reward, or become the president of the United States are fantasies that are quite easy to detect. Let's say we are fantasizing about having nice weather and going for a walk. We imagine that it's going to be very peaceful, that we are going to sit on the beach or in a cool forest. Perhaps we are going to have a wonderful meditation experience or meet all kinds of interesting people. Then it turns out that the weather is very rainy and we can't go out at all. If we are living in that egoic mind, if we can't accept change, then we can experience a tremendous sense of disappointment. That's quite familiar to all of us, right? We all know that we have been victimized by the demon of fantasy. We remember much of our life being enslaved by our unfulfilled fantasies.

When we realize that *everything* is a fantasy, things change. From the perspective of this truth we are no longer lost in agony or grief. But when we are not in that mind, when something we were counting on turns out to be a fantasy, we experience disappointment and anger. When we realize that everything is a fantasy there is no self shouting or reacting to our true circumstances in life. I am not saying don't fantasize about anything, not at all. It's impossible anyway. This is not about blocking our consciousness. It's not about trying not to fantasize. This is not about suppressing or shutting down our consciousness. This isn't about trying to not feel, or not think, or not fantasize. It is about realizing the difference between fantasy and reality.

All of us have fantasies. Fantasies can be very beautiful. Our consciousness needs fantasies sometimes and it is okay to have them as long as we don't believe in them. As long as we realize that these fantasies are fantasies. But it is hard to distinguish what is fantasy and what is real when we have succumbed to this egoic, unenlightened mind.

When we meditate we begin to realize that not even one phenomenon, one condition in life, is a concrete reality. It turns out that each and every condition, each and every phenomenon in this outer world is a fantasy. We don't accept this because we are afraid that this is going to bring tremendous grief and agony. We are working very hard most of the time trying to prevent conditions from becoming a fantasy. We are fighting very hard each and every moment trying to gain authority over reality in order to prevent all of our imagined conditions from becoming fantasy. We don't like to see it as fantasy because fantasy means unreal, mind projected. I, or my ego perhaps, is truly working very hard to prevent me from realizing that I am also a fantasy. The self is a fantasy too, you see.

Perhaps the worst thing that you can say to somebody is that something is their fantasy. "Hey, it's your fantasy." It's easy for us to be offended when somebody says that. But that is exactly what the truth is telling us. "It's your fantasy." I think truth's mantra is "It's your fantasy." When we feel like we are suffering, it's our fantasy. When we feel that we are awakening, it is our fantasy. When we feel that something is wrong with our life, it's the same, our fantasy. That's what the truth is always shouting and uttering as an eternal mantra because the truth has only one intention and that is to awaken all of us. So its divine eternal mantra is "Hey, it's your fantasy." That's all it is saying in each and every moment.

But don't try to get rid of the fantasy. That's a fantasy too. When we try to get rid of this fantasy we wind up being very frustrated because it doesn't work ultimately. So this is not really about getting rid of fantasy. When we allow our mind to become one with the truth or in agreement with the truth we realize without any effort that everything is a fantasy. The realization that all phenomena are a fantasy comes to us. We see it so clearly. Therefore all that we need to do is simply meditate. If we keep meditating, we realize that everything is a fantasy.

If we want to realize the truth, the first thing to remember is that we don't have to do anything. No sacred dances. No secret mantras. No religious conversion. We just sit quietly wherever we find ourselves and simply don't do anything. This is most important. Don't do anything.

We look directly and see what is true in that moment without labeling or judging anything. Now we see the truth which is beyond our fantasies. We also see that our mind is a conglomeration of mental events, fleeting and insubstantial. At that moment it's impossible to become attached to any personal story line. This is a perfect moment. It lacks nothing. That recognition brings about a sense of inexhaustible joy. We might feel like we want to get up and dance wildly. If so, do it and call it sacred dance.

CHAPTER NINE

Are We on the Right Track?

Compassion and Loving-Kindness

NOW AND THEN we wonder whether we are on the right track or not. We ask ourselves this question from time to time, not every day. We can't afford to ask it every day because it might spoil our day. Like that, sometimes when we are in our car headed someplace, we drive for a while and then we start wondering whether we are going in the right direction or not. It can be a little uncomfortable but still it's very good to ask the question, "Am I on the right track or not?"

Ultimately there is no guarantee that we're definitely on the right track. Some people may use their affiliation with a religious organization to validate that they're on the right path. However, in general, spiritual traditions sometimes work like clothes made for a baby or small child. Sooner or later, if we spiritually evolve, we'll outgrow them the same way babies outgrow their clothes. If we try to keep ourselves swaddled in religious tradition, we'll soon become uncomfortable and constricted. Eventually we have to go beyond all conventional forms just like Buddha went beyond all conventional forms in his inner awakening. Then we'll become like space which cannot be bound by anything, and our religion will be truth and love. Until that happens, there is no guarantee that we're on the right track.

It is easy to hold on to the psychological comfort that comes from association with isms in any form. But we have to be intelligent; we have to distinguish mere psychological comfort from a true spiritual path. To do this we must invite doubt. Please invite doubt and be aware that there are two kinds of doubt. One is detrimental to our inner progress and the other is helpful to our inner progress. There is a form of doubt that is based on fear and mistrust. This kind of doubt often keeps us from plumbing the depths of the truth. It pulls us away and prevents us from surrendering. If we're thirsty for the cup of nectar in front of us, we might hear our mind whispering, "Be careful. This might not be nectar after all." If we listen to this, we close our lips and turn away. That is the wrong kind of doubt because it stops us. Benevolent doubt fosters a form of courageous inquiry. It has the yearning to realize the truth and it encourages further exploration.

I am not recommending that people have this doubt constantly. Still it is necessary to ask the question now and again, "Am I on the right track or not?" It's easy to think we're on the right track simply because outwardly we're following a spiritual path or a spiritual teacher. But that is not a guarantee. That is not enough to ensure that we are on the right track. We can be spiritual seekers and at the same time we can be very ordinary in terms of perpetuating our own karmic patterns of anger, hatred, and judgment. Being spiritual seekers does not mean that we have eternal certainty or assurance that we are on the right track and therefore don't have to inquire into the very nature of our motivation. Why are we on the path in the first place? Where are we heading? What is our motivation? Are we looking for another form of security? Are we seeking another belief system? Are we looking for a sense of security? It's possible we have ulterior motives such as these.

Ego is always looking for security but security is an illusion ultimately. As soon as we encounter a crisis our sense of security is shattered. But we don't allow ourselves to remain in a state of unknowing; we immediately latch on to the next thing, whatever promises security. We are just like a monkey who jumps off one branch of a tree and then immediately jumps onto another branch.

Ego is always fantasizing about security. Not just security but eternal security. Ego is going around the universe looking for eternal security. So far it has not been found because eternal security is an illusion. There is no security in this world after all. Ego has the misperception that controlling reality will make us secure. It wants security because the opposite of security is no security and that basically means death, impermanence, and getting things we don't want. Ego thinks that we have to constantly make an effort to control reality. Usually we're deeply insecure when we are looking for security. If we are insecure inside, then our heart is closed and we are not ready to express a transcendental level of love and compassion. Enlightenment is not security. However, many people end up on the spiritual path with a hope for ultimate security because they are insecure about the future, about the unknown.

Is there ultimate security? If we don't check our motives carefully, it's possible that we are hoping that enlightenment will be our final safe harbor, a place where everything is hunky dory. Enlightenment is not some kind of eternal security. Enlightenment does not insure that everything is going to be fine from that moment on. It does not insure that Buddha or God is always going to smile upon us. When we are enlightened we still have to die. We still get sick. We still get annoyed from time to time. We still experience all of life's conditions just as everyone else experiences life's conditions. The difference is that we no longer have strong, ordinary compulsive reactions to these situations in terms of liking and disliking them. Such reactions often produce hatred, attachment, aversion, desire, and so forth. Enlightenment is not security. It is freedom from both security and insecurity.

Sooner or later we have to give up security. This is our assignment.

We have to give up any illusion of security. In the Buddhist teachings sometimes we deliberately practice visualizations and meditations in which we invite all the kinds of security that ego desires, whatever that means: permanent youth, relationships, anything we are attached to. Youth is sometimes very comforting when we are living in this ordinary unenlightened realm. Youth is worshipped, so think about youth. It is quite possible to have a very strong compulsive attachment to being young. But youth is an illusion because it doesn't last forever. Eventually we all age. Sometimes it is powerful to visualize ourselves getting older. There is a whole set of meditation practices where we visualize ourselves being very old, very sick, and eventually dying. We can visualize that our body is being burned in a fire or being chopped into tiny pieces and fed to hungry vultures as they do in the charnel grounds in Tibet. It is a very powerful visualization in terms of accentuating all unreasonable attachment to youth and being young. It is also a way of cutting through attachment to this quest for security and permanence.

Think about security in terms of relationships, relationships between men and women, teachers and students, between groups, countries, and so forth. We see that these relationships are impermanent. There really is no ultimate security in relationships. Think about money, success, and career. In those areas things are always changing. Nothing is permanent. Everything is appearing and disappearing. Everything in this entire existence is the miraculous dance of divine truth. The truth is always dancing. It never takes a break. The truth is dancing day and night, eternally from the very beginning without any end. Everything is manifested in this dance. The dance is not static. It is constantly in motion, appearing and disappearing, coming together and moving away. So if we are not ready to accept the truth that this existence is always in motion, always changeable, always transient, then we have a big problem. We have a problem not just with ourselves. We have a problem with the truth. You know sometimes people say, "I have a problem with my neighbor." That is nothing compared to having a problem with the truth. People have problems with their car or with the president. That's okay. Imagine that we have a problem with reality. Now we really have a big problem.

If we look carefully into our mind from this perspective, we realize that we have a serious problem with the truth. We do not accept the transient quality of existence. We do not accept it at all. Most often we see change as the ultimate state of danger. Ego is constantly trying to escape from accepting and embracing that eternal dancelike transient quality of existence. Ego doesn't like that dance. Ego hates the divine dance more than anything else. Ego loves things that exist and become solid like a rock. Not just a rock but an eternal, unchangeable rock. No changes, everything secure.

On the spiritual path first we inquire. We look and begin to see the very nature of our suffering. Where has suffering originated? Where does suffering come from? Is it from the outside, from physical situations such as birth, sickness, old age, and death? Is it from not getting what we want? Or is it generated from within our own consciousness? Through the lens of introspection we will come to realize that all of our suffering, major as well as minor, originates within our unenlightened consciousness. It comes from the fact that we do not accept the nature of existence. We do not accept the fact that everything is changeable, always transient and always in motion. If we allow our ego to be the master, if we allow our ego to dominate our consciousness and control our response to the way things are, then we see things as fundamentally dark and polarized. We feel that we have to fight constantly to maintain a sense of security. We feel that we are in this fight constantly whether we are sitting, walking, sleeping, or waking. We feel that there is always a war happening somewhere in our consciousness. This lack of peace is what Buddha called dukkha, or existential anguish. It is always there. Sometimes we are conscious of it but most of the time we are not conscious of it. It does not mean we are not experiencing that dukkha when we are not conscious of it. Sometimes we are able to manage being unconscious of this suffering. We do this by distracting our mind through enjoying sensual pleasures, keeping busy, fantasizing about beautiful futures, and so on.

When we truly realize that this war is happening we become more aware and we don't have to fight so much. We don't have to try to change or control things. We don't have to try to perform this huge feng shui on the universe. Sometimes we are like feng shui masters for the universe. We try to rearrange everything—sun here, moon here, I'm in the center, get rid of old age and death. How about that? That's what we are trying to do most of the time. No old age. Let's add more to the list. We are trying to maintain everlasting youth and everlasting pleasure. We are really working hard on that project, aren't we?

Eventually we have to realize the truth. Things are impermanent. Things are not under our control. We have to tell ourselves, "This is the truth. You must accept it." At first ego says, "I don't like this truth. I can't allow this truth." Then we give it a few days. Then ego says, "This is too much for me to handle right now. Leave me alone and I'll think about it. I may change my mind." So now there is ego but there is also this kind of weak, wimpy awareness arising. And this wimpy awareness tells ego, "This is the truth. Please accept it." And they talk.

Ego says, "Oh, no! I'm not going to accept that. That cannot be the truth. Truth should be something else. Truth should be according to my definition of what is true." For ego that means that now there is a possibility that we can control reality. There is the possibility that we can rearrange the universe the way we want it. More than that there is the possibility of controlling everything while being on the spiritual path and searching for truth. How could it be more convenient?

The more we meditate the stronger awareness becomes. That is the power of sincere inquiry. Awareness gets stronger and stronger and eventually ego becomes weaker and weaker. Resistance becomes weaker and weaker. Soon we realize that awareness is completely occupying our body, mind, spirit, and heart. Now we are completely in alignment with truth. Finally we have accepted the true nature of all things. That is inner liberation. In that acceptance there is great bliss because with it we are finally free from a self-imposed prison of ignorance.

We must practice becoming aware of the layers of all our motives and we should apply this practice to all aspects of our life. People sometimes get married for security. When that is the case then sometimes, after a while, they might not be so happy about the promises made in their wedding vows. People may find that they betray themselves by seeking security without considering their true needs. Wrong motivation often leads to an undesired result. Even on the spiritual path we can still be subject to these wrong motives. Now instead of mundane desires, we turn toward God or guru to find the ultimate level of security. That's why people can be very defensive about their religion. It can manifest as blind faith in the infallibility of their spiritual authority. We just don't want to let go of security at any cost.

What happens if we just let go? Nothing happens except inner liberation. There is still food on the table. We are still brushing our teeth in the morning. Ultimately nothing can go wrong. It's all perfect as it is. If we are dying in the moment, it's still perfect as it is. All is being taken care of in the realm of perfection. That realm is what reality truly is. There is a story about a man who traveled in the mountains and was overtaken by nightfall. As he continued walking in the dim light, he fell over what seemed to him to be a steep cliff. He managed to grab onto the branches of a small bush. He was holding on to it for dear life, imagining in his mind sure death if he let go of it. He spent the whole night in agony. By the first light of morning, sapped of all his strength, he lost his grip and fell. He was surprised to find that he landed on a secure ledge just two feet below where he had been clinging to the branches for dear life. This humorous story illustrates our irrational fear and obsession. Because of our irrational fear we feel we must be in control. This originates from our belief that there is something fundamentally wrong with reality. The truth is that security is unobtainable because it is the very fabric of reality. Reality is all-pervading. We can never fall out of it. We are already secure and we are always secure. Searching for security is our biggest neurosis. It keeps us deluded. All modes of striving for security are forms of fear and obsession and our heart cannot be open as long as we're ruled by them. Compassion and love can only arise from an open heart. To see if we're on the right track, look at the measure of love and compassion we express in our life.

I remember listening to the teachings of a Tibetan lama recently. He was so kind. He never really criticized anybody. He was talking about terrorists but he never called them terrorists. He simply called them mischievous people. Many great spiritual teachers have said that if your mind is completely engrossed in compassion, then we can be one hundred percent confident that we are on the right track. If we are able to hold everyone in our heart, if we are able to love everyone without any discrimination, that means that we are on the right track. It doesn't matter whether we have knowledge about Buddhism or not, whether we are intellectually sophisticated or not, whether we are a beginner or not. We know that we are on the right track because our heart is blessed by compassion and loving-kindness.

On the other hand if our heart is becoming bitter, angry, judgmental, and arrogant, if we are creating unnecessary separation between ourselves and others, if we are becoming sectarian, thinking that we are better than others, thinking that we are part of a "chosen people," that means that something is not working with our spiritual practice. Therefore it is always good to double check. When we realize that our heart is hardened by judgment and separation, then we must pray. Pray to the truth. Pray for our heart to be blessed, to be opened. And our heart will always be opened because we are praying to the truth that is most exalted. Ultimately we are praying to what is always residing within us. Truth is always residing in us, day and night, in each and every moment. Our heart is the hidden paradise. Sooner or later we have to find the golden key and open the door to that hidden paradise inside. If we are looking for a paradise outside of our consciousness, then we'll be wandering endlessly in this realm of illusion.

So we have to remember eventually that there is a hidden, enchanted paradise, our heart. That is the land of bliss, this pure consciousness that is very loving and forgiving, that does not know how to judge us or anybody else. It is always ready to bless us. Actually it is already granting a shower of blessings.

We are hiding under this shell of ego, protecting ourselves from that divine rain. We are afraid of that rain because it is going to destroy all of our illusions. So we are hiding constantly under the shell of ego, trying to escape from the divine shower. We are being blessed in each and every moment so we don't have to do anything ultimately. We don't have to go anywhere. All we have to do is come out of that shell called ego and let ourselves take a break. Let ourselves take a break from this judgmental, angry, hateful ego. Then we will experience our true nature, compassion and loving-kindness.

Ultimately life is very short. Even if we live one hundred years more, that is still very short. We don't have time to hate anybody. We don't have time to judge anybody. So how are we going to spend the rest of our life from this moment on? This is a good question. "How am I going to spend the rest of my life from this moment on?" We must realize that life is extremely short. It is like the snap of our fingers until the time that we die. So we have to realize that ultimately there is nothing to gain and nothing to lose. Ultimately there are no enemies, there are no friends. There is not even any "I." From this moment on, the only thing that matters is to live life from compassion, awareness, and wisdom. And when we decide that, then our heart opens and we experience being in bliss. No matter what is happening outside we are still able to experience inner bliss because we are able to see that every situation in life is the divine dance of truth. There is no longer an "I" who is constantly fighting against and trying to control the expression of reality. Enlightenment blossoms naturally within.

When we are able to go beyond all internal obscurations such as pride, judgment, and fear, we are finally able to be in touch with the very original primordial nature of our consciousness, and that is love and compassion. Love is the ability to see every circumstance and every being as perfect just as they are. That's love. Love is devotion. Love is seeing that everybody is divine. It is the total acceptance of all things. That state is free from conflict.

There is a little bit of a difference between love and compassion. Compassion is an expression of love. Compassion is like having sympathy for the suffering of all living beings. Sometimes when we see the suffering of others we spontaneously experience compassion. Remember, love is our ability to see everybody as divine. From the place of all-embracing love, we are able to effortlessly experience compassion toward all beings who are suffering, who are in a state of turmoil. It would be very difficult to have pure compassion toward others unless we recognize their true nature as divine. When we are able to let go of our identification with the small self, then we automatically experience that we are love, that we are compassion. It's just like the sun when it rises above the clouds, then it shines very brilliantly and illuminates all darkness.

One time two people had an assignment to assassinate a politician. They went to his home and waited for him to show up. Usually he came home at seven o'clock every night, but on this day at seven o'clock he wasn't there. Nine, ten, eleven o'clock and still he didn't show up. It got to be midnight and still the politician wasn't home. Finally the would-be assassins looked at each other and one of them said, "I'm getting a little worried. I hope he's okay." So this person experienced his divine nature right there and forgot that he was the assassin. He forgot that the politician was supposed to be the enemy. He lost all of his concepts so he was in touch with his true nature. The only thing he experienced was caring and loving-kindness.

As human beings, we are inherently good. Not in the sense that we are always on our best behavior according to some conventional moral code. We are good because we are already truth, love, and beauty. When we are free from all inner conditioning we are awakened to our true being and we see that we are all utterly divine.

CHAPTER TEN

Shortcut to Enlightenment
Transcending Thoughts

⟶

Fɪʀsᴛ ᴡᴇ ʜᴀᴠᴇ to come to believe that enlightenment is possible. We must know that each of us can glimpse enlightenment at any given moment, whenever we are ready. Great masters have said this many, many times and we should take them at their word. We must believe this idea that enlightenment is possible at any given moment. But when we are completely wrapped up in the powerful forces of our emotions, concepts, and habitual patterns, we find it difficult to open our mind to such a possibility. I want to remind everybody that enlightenment is more than possible. Enlightenment is always knocking on our door. This is not just some kind of optimistic Buddhist good news. This is the truth.

There is no need to mystify this truth. However, ego is always working hard to prevent enlightenment. Whenever we are mystifying the truth either individually or collectively, it is the work of the ego or, as the Christians might say, the work of the devil. There is only one enlightenment and it is the same enlightenment that Buddha Shakyamuni realized. Yet there have been conflicting theories about what enlightenment is.

First we have to go beyond theories no matter how sacred they might seem. Theories can create an illusory distance between us and enlightenment. This manifests in two ways. When we believe enlightenment is far away this can lead to discouragement. It's like being asked to climb to the top of Mount Everest. It's just too much, impossible. The second thing that happens is that we can become involved in chasing after enlightenment like a child chases after a rainbow. This leads nowhere no matter how relentless our effort.

So why are we not awakened right now? What force holds us back from awakening to the ultimate truth? It often seems that there are huge obstacles. But when we look into our consciousness and simply ask what is holding us back, we don't really find anything. We don't find a devil with two horns holding us back. I always say that it would be good news if we found such a devil. Then we could all get together and wrestle it. That would be easy. But there is no devil. There is nothing outside of our consciousness holding us back from being awake right now. There are no real blocks, no hindrances. Let me tell you this Buddhist story.

One time a husband told his wife that she could not have any relationships after he died. "If you do, I am going to manifest as a powerful demon and make your life hell." So when the domineering husband died the wife took his words seriously for months and years. Finally she kind of forgot and started having relationships with other people. Whenever she came home from a date, however, this demon popped up on her ceiling. He looked very fierce. Flames were coming out of his mouth. He yelled, "You went out. You had a date." The demon was real. It knew the exact clothes her date was wearing. It knew their exact height and so forth. She was terrified and consulted a Buddhist master. This master told her to carry a handful of rice. He told her that the next time the demon appeared to ask it just one question: "Ask it to tell you how many grains of rice are in your hand." So the next time this demon popped up she grabbed a handful of rice and yelled, "If you are so omniscient, tell me right now how many grains of rice are in my hand?" Instantly the demon disappeared and never came back. Of course you know that the demon was actually her creation. It was in her mind. The story demonstrates that everything is the elaboration of our own mind.

When we start inquiring into what is holding us back from realizing the truth we come to the realization that there is really nothing there. There are no obstacles. Nothing is holding us back from awakening. That is very amazing to see and this is a shortcut to enlightenment. We are the only one not allowing ourselves to be free. We are the only one who can set ourselves free. We are the one who imprisons and we are the one who liberates. When we accept that responsibility we have finally gained spiritual maturity. That maturity is required in order to be fully enlightened and once it is realized we are ready to go.

If we are still wondering how to awaken, I suggest that we meditate now and then and focus on the following question: "What is holding me back from realizing my true nature, my Buddha Nature?" This is a very powerful inquiry. I am sharing this based on my own meditation practice. This is one of my favorite meditations because it always takes me to the place where I cannot blame anybody or anything for my lack of awakening.

When we open our hearts and let go of all of our theories and speculations, when we are not distracted even by spiritual fantasies, when we simply wholeheartedly and courageously inquire into what is holding us back, that is all that we need to do. Sometimes it is good when we are by ourselves to just take off our clothes and shout loudly to the sky, "Who is holding me back from awakening right now?" Or we can just ask the truth, "What is holding me back from awakening right now?" Either way we can't find any answer because there is nobody there. There is nothing holding us back and that's why we never really find any answers.

If anybody tells us that they have the answer, they are obviously lying because there isn't any answer. Next we might ask, "If there are no obstacles holding me back, then why am I not awakened right now?" And when we look we realize that we are attached to our thoughts. That's all that is happening. Samsara is nothing more than our identification with thoughts. That's all there is. There is nothing there except thoughts.

I met with a veteran of the Vietnam War many years ago in a small town in Louisiana. He was quite moved by my teachings. He was crying and he said that he felt guilty about being in the war. He felt that he was a sinner without any possibility of redemption. He asked me what he should do. He asked if I had anything to say. I couldn't come up with any words right there. So I sat there for a while and meditated and prayed. Finally the words that came out of my mouth from that prayer were, "Actually that was in the past. You must live in the present. This is not about condoning your deeds. I am not saying that your activity was great or noble. But in the ultimate sense there is only your own identification with thoughts and ideas, guilt, and shame. Let go of it. You have the capacity to be free right now in this very moment." And so I think that this person got my message for the time being. He had a smile on his face. I never met him after that. I always hoped that he took that message to heart.

When we look into our consciousness we recognize that our heart has been tormented pretty much throughout our entire lifetime. Our heart has always been tormented. Perhaps it has never been completely at peace in our entire life. That often is the foundation of our relationship with each other. We come together because our hearts have been tormented and we are looking for a sense of liberation, an answer to how we can transcend the internal pain and confusion that is always there. That is why we attend spiritual teachings, why we attend workshops, why we go to retreats, and why we try all kinds of methods and all kinds of special practices. We do it in order to find a sense of liberation and freedom from that inner torment. Our heart has never been completely at peace, completely enlightened, completely serene. If we look into our hearts right now, we see that there is a lot of ancient baggage, pain, sorrow, and confusion. But at the same time there is really nothing there except thoughts.

Imagine that your heart is tormented by hatred. Imagine that we hate somebody because we believe they hurt us when we were a child. That seems to be a universal problem in the Western world. Many people have a tremendous sense of anger and hatred toward their parents. This was a shocking discovery for me when I first came to the United States. Many people experience a sense of rage and very strong anger toward their parents and other people who hurt them. Ultimately that is also a thought. It doesn't exist anymore in this very pure present moment. It doesn't really exist. So actually what we are really carrying is nothing but a bunch of thoughts. When we let go of those thoughts then nothing else is required. We are free.

Think about being poor. Think that you are very poor. Start believing that you are very poor. We can really torture ourselves with these thoughts. "I don't have a nice car. My neighbor's house is much nicer than my house. I really don't have many of the things that I need." Then we can try to get more money and have a better this and that. We can use all of our energy trying to acquire more money, more lucrative work, and so forth. Still we find that our heart is tormented even after we have gained an abundance of material things. That proves that no matter how hard we try to modify the outer circumstances of our life, it never resolves our problems. If we are able to transcend and let go of our concept that we are poor, then we are free from that imaginary problem right there. Our true nature goes beyond being poor and being rich.

Whenever you suffer, whenever you struggle, don't go outside trying to find out what is wrong with your life. Don't treat your life like you treat your car. When something is wrong with the car we get out, open the hood, see what's wrong with the engine, and fix it. But life is not like a car. Life is consciousness. Life is not something outside of us. Therefore whenever we feel that we are suffering, tormented, or challenged we should always look into our consciousness. Immediately we discover that we are having a very evil affair with an evil thought. That's all there is. Just that thought.

Such thoughts always come with a specific idea and with some kind of voice: "I am good. I am bad. I am poor. I don't have this or that. I am not enlightened." It is always associated with a concept and a belief system. Until we are awakened to the ultimate truth we are completely ruled by our thoughts. Thoughts are always dictating reality to us. So in that sense thought is the ultimate empire of propaganda. Thought is always coloring and defining reality.

I went back to Tibet about ten years ago. People there have very few possessions or material wealth. They have almost nothing. Yet inside, many of them are completely wealthy. I brought all of these presents from the United States and then I was hesitant to give them out because many of the people are so pure and so happy. I felt that maybe I was going to pollute their minds. I didn't want to trap their minds because some of the people are so openhearted, loving, and completely rich.

I have met with some very wealthy people the last few years in the United States, and when I looked into their faces they were very unhappy. Yet when I looked into the faces of some of those very sincere, good-hearted people living in the countryside in Tibet, who have absolute devotion to the path of loving-kindness and wisdom, I saw that their hearts were very rich, completely rich. Strangely enough somebody over there who had almost nothing is one hundred times happier than someone over here with millions of dollars. So that really shows that ultimately nothing is really wrong with life.

There are only two realms we can reside in. One is called nirvana— that is enlightenment. The other is called samsara—the unenlightened world, which is basically the state of our own consciousness. Samsara is not out there even though we often project it outside. This is why we are in conflict with reality. Our ego always tries to conquer reality and that effort itself is the basis of our misery. So if we stop fighting with reality and look inside, we will discover that samsara is in each of us. Then we realize that samsara is the state where we are attached to our thoughts. Even death is a thought. This may be considered quite unconventional because it does not go along with consensual reality. But consensual reality is actually a reality determined by collective ignorance. If we take a moment to transcend all of our thoughts, we realize that nirvana lies within us and that it is totally inexpressible.

When we suffer it means that we are attached to a thought. When we feel happy that means that we are experiencing another thought. The very sense of "I" is a thought too. The "I" that I believe to be so real and concrete doesn't exist in the ultimate sense. It is just a thought. It is a thought that I have been defending my entire lifetime; a thought that I am willing to defend for the rest of my life. Quite deluded isn't it? "I" is just a thought and yet I am constantly worrying about the well-being of this "I." Is it getting enough sleep? Is it getting enough food? Does it have health insurance? How are its teeth? Has it had a checkup with the dentist? Does it have a nice hairstyle?

The most liberating, most blissful awareness that you can experience is that "I" is a lie. Now and then we realize that and it is so liberating. Of course it doesn't happen too often. Perhaps you have had such a liberating experience. Sometimes those realizations happen when we are in the presence of somebody who is living in that awareness or when we do a lot of silent meditation.

Our true nature has always been perfect. It doesn't have to be improved and it never can be changed. It is the wonder of wonders. It is intrinsically divine. We don't always experience it because our thoughts and impulses are obscuring it. Practicing meditation means working toward transcending those thoughts each and every moment.

Sometimes it is good to even recite lines, special mantras, to help us to remember to maintain awareness. Awareness is a state in which those thoughts are transcended.

People often talk about transcending life and death. That's a lofty ideal isn't it? People also talk about transcending samsara and that's lofty too. How can we transcend samsara when there is no samsara? So just forget about trying to transcend samsara and life and death. Please forget all these fantastic, glorious, heroic notions because they suggest enlightenment is totally beyond human achievement. They deliberately make things more difficult than they actually are. There is no samsara. There is no life and death to transcend in the first place. The only thing that we must transcend is our thoughts. Beyond our own thoughts there is no suffering. There is only thought.

This is not simply theory. But what does it mean to transcend our thoughts? It simply means not to believe in our thoughts. When we don't believe in our thoughts we are always awakened. When we believe in our thoughts we are unawakened. That's a statement everybody should memorize. Whenever we are suffering we should tell ourselves, "I am stuck with my thoughts." Then we might like to pray and ask for help. Ask for the power to transcend our thoughts. Ultimately transcending thoughts means not to believe in the thoughts.

This is a perfect moment for everybody to surrender their thoughts, to give up all thoughts, surrender them to the truth. We can offer all of our thoughts whenever we have the mindfulness and awareness. In temples we have a shrine room and the altars are arranged with offering bowls filled with water, flowers, rice, and so forth as symbols of the ultimate offering. The ultimate offering is thought. Offering all thoughts to emptiness without any attachment is the highest offering. Every time we offer thought to that realm of truth we always experience blissful awakening.

In our consciousness there is a dance of thoughts happening. There is no need to get rid of them. But if we pay attention we see that we are very familiar with all of these thoughts. They are our neighbors and roommates. They are the habitual patterns of our consciousness. They keep following and chasing us as though they had their own life force. When we are attached to our thoughts the thoughts become crystallized and turn into a cloud of concepts and belief systems, which are the chains which bind us to inner suffering.

Imagine that we are playing this game of blocking our eyes with our hands while we are in a beautiful flower garden. As soon as we unblock our eyes we are able to see the beautiful flowers, lotuses, lilies, sunflowers, and so forth. But when we block our eyes again the blackout returns again and we don't see the beautiful flowers although they are still there. Our relationship with thoughts is just like that. When our mind is free from thoughts we can see the beautiful truth; when our mind is veiled by thoughts then we don't see that beautiful truth which is always there.

The Buddha and great masters such as Nagarjuna, Shantideva, and Machig Labdron have always been illuminating the true path to enlightenment. Their message has always been uncompromisingly simple and straightforward. They have been teaching us to go beyond all of our belief systems. And yet there is a way that we can keep avoiding such deliverance because our mind has a stubborn propensity to grasp at thoughts and impulses. Our spiritual practice should be about freeing everything that is stuck in our consciousness.

However, we may discover that our spiritual practice is about gathering more information, more knowledge, more security, especially this sense of security. So it is good to review the very nature of our practice and see whether it is about transcending our thoughts or not. Do not believe in your mind. Do not believe in your thoughts. When we no longer believe in this mind we experience ultimate freedom within. We are always free since there is no suffering, there is no death, there is no illness, and there is no old age to be transcended in the first place. Such freedom is universal and it is our birthright.

What are we waiting for? This is the moment to let go of all of our doubt and fear. This is the moment to jump through the door to that paradise of eternal freedom. When we know how to go beyond our thoughts without procrastination then we have acquired the precious knowledge that is the shortcut to enlightenment.

CHAPTER ELEVEN

Nonattachment

Going Beyond All Limitations

F OR A HUMAN BEING the highest aspiration is to realize the state
of utter transcendence, going beyond all limitations. If this is the
reason we embark on a spiritual path, we are headed in the right direction. This basic aspiration is pure in itself, even though as time goes by
it gets mixed up with all sorts of reasons and motivations. This aspiration is a powerful force, like falling madly in love. Actually, it is falling
in love. We fall in love with truth, that eternal freedom. In spiritual circles we often hear the word "devotion," but this is the only true devotion, one which will help us to wake up from samsara.

In the East many people call this life samsara, which means having an existence that is doomed to unending disappointment. Millions
of people are seeking a way out of it. There has been a long tradition
of practicing even severe austerities in order to be free from it. Those
methods included tormenting the body by flagellation, fasting, and
other extreme measures. The view of those engaged in these practices
is that life is full of sorrow and the body is sinful. The unique aspect
of Buddha's approach is the middle way, which teaches that samsara is

not the fault of the body or life in general. Samsara is a state of ignorant mind.

We often project samsara out onto circumstances. When something goes wrong in our life we tend to look upon life as meaningless drudgery, a joyless struggle. Our outlook becomes pessimistic. Our hearts get bitter and we become angry at everything around us. We blame everybody, including God, for our misfortune. In the modern world we blame our parents for all of our problems even though most parents do their best. Actually, all of the problems we fight against do not really exist. They are only fabrications of our unenlightened mind.

One of our biggest problems is the idea of death. Even that doesn't exist because there has never been anybody there to die in the first place. This sense of "I" is a grand illusion. Life without this illusion is truly beautiful. Without this illusion we feel that we have much love and joy to share with everyone in the world.

Sometimes I meet with idealistic people who are disillusioned with their life and trying to find meaning through escapism. But as long as we are not free within, no matter where we go we will find plenty of problems. Most of our problems are a product of our mind. Once we truly realize this fact, we have the freedom to choose between misery and happiness. The natural state of our being is always perfectly happy. Happiness and freedom are our birthright. Searching for happiness and freedom outside of ourselves is always a mistake from the start.

It is said that when Buddha became awakened, he realized mahanirvana, the state where there is not even a nirvana to be found. After that, he never lost his awakened mind. That is the enlightenment that Buddha realized. He stopped searching for anything from that moment on. He went beyond everything. As the *Prajnaparamita Sutra* says, "There is no attainment, there is no nonattainment." Attainment is just an idea in the ultimate sense. Who is trying to attain something in the first place? Who is there? What is to be attained? Once we go beyond duality these ideas lose their meaning right there. Enlightenment and delusion are two sides of the same coin. That coin is the big ignorance that gives rise to this illusion of separation. Truth itself is the oneness of all things.

In some sense there is enlightenment and there is no enlightenment. This is not a contradictory statement. There is enlightenment, of course, because there is freedom and liberation. But there is no enlightenment when we are desperately searching for it someplace outside of ourselves. Look. Who is searching for enlightenment? If we bring about awareness in our mind right now, we see that it is the same "I" who searches for everything. Who is searching for fame? Who is searching for pleasure? Who is searching for a way to arrive at the truth? It is the same "I." The "I" who is searching for enlightenment is the same "I." This "I" is sometimes very holy and sometimes extremely nasty. You see, this "I" has a big closet filled with all kinds of masks. There are masks of being holy and masks of being quite sinister. The "I" who wants to wring somebody's neck is the same "I" who is searching for enlightenment. You see, it's all the business of "I." There is no good "I." There is no bad "I." There is only one "I" and it's called the ego. Ego is a mental construct, a fabrication. It has nothing to do with who we really are.

The very heart of the matter is that all of our problems, of course, are the creation of this "I." It is a realm of habits and karmic propensities that we have been investing in for countless eons. We are all carrying a big rucksack of internal stuff in our minds, wherever we go, whatever we do. Now and then, we have a deep aspiration to put it down. First, we have to know that this burden is not part of us. It doesn't belong to us. Realizing that this is so is the act of putting it down. That is the only true spiritual practice there is. Everything else we do is mere distraction. Like child's play it is designed to amuse us for a while. Lots of spiritual practices don't help us. Instead they contribute to that burden with holier stuff. This is nothing more than decorating our chain with beautiful, glittering gems. This is the reason why Buddha rejected all of the spiritual discipline that was there during his time. He engaged in a path of giving up identification with this false sense of "I," what we call "ego."

In general, as time goes by our mental habits keep growing like weeds. They grow like a rolling snowball until they are transcended from their root. Meditation is a way of stopping that rolling snowball. We have so many habits of fear, hatred, and judgment, habits of violence and aggression. In fact we have so many of these habits that we should not expect that meditation is going to be an ecstatic journey. In the beginning meditation can be very challenging and quite annoying. I often say that in the beginning meditation is like opening the septic tank of a very large city.

These days, people often go to resort areas where they have massages and hot tubs, yoga and meditation. People think that meditation is a way of relaxing their body and mind. They think it is a way of rejuvenating themselves, a way of removing wrinkles from their foreheads. They think that they will be eternally attractive because of meditation. But this is not what meditation is all about.

Meditation is not a stress reduction program. Of course there is nothing wrong with using meditation as a way of reducing stress and anxiety. That is much healthier than taking intoxicating substances or turning oneself into a zombie in front of the TV or becoming unconscious by stuffing oneself with ice cream. This reduces stress but not in a healthy way. But reducing stress is not the whole point of meditation; it is a bit of a watered-down version. Meditation has a very special purpose. Meditation is a way of transcending everything. There are many ways of reducing stress. Go to the beach! Go to the spa! You will get relaxed. Of course I am not trying to stop you from attending those stress reduction programs based on meditation. They are very healthy. But that is not the whole point.

Meditation must challenge you. Ask yourself, "Is my meditation challenging me?" If the answer is yes, it means that you are getting somewhere. But if your spiritual practice is simply soothing you, it means that something is not working. This is a red flag. There is a big problem. Spirituality should not be like a teddy bear. It should not be a touchy-feely experience where beautiful, sentimental feelings arise. Sometimes people say, "Oh, I love this meditation because it's very soothing. I love this meditation practice because it relaxes me." Challenge has to take place in our consciousness. The true path must challenge the very core of our reality. It must challenge every concept about who we are and what our reality is. Meditating is like inviting fire into our consciousness. That is what true meditation is all about. Otherwise all of our problems are still in one piece while we are the best meditators on the planet. Without challenge nothing really happens in our consciousness. Our meditation will produce no more results than nibbling on candy. Nibbling on candy makes us feel very good sometimes but nothing is happening in our consciousness. We are still unconscious while we are great meditators.

So what is meditation all about? Actually meditation begins with a true aspiration to just let go of everything. Remember that the definition of Dharma, the purpose of following the spiritual path, is nonattachment. There is a line in Buddhist literature:

There WAS no attachment.
There IS no attachment.
There WILL BE no attachment.

Seen from this view, meditation is very profound and yet very simple.

Have you ever ridden a bicycle? The bicycle does not run on its own. The bicycle runs only when somebody is pedaling it. The moment we stop pedaling the bicycle, it falls over. Unenlightened consciousness works in the same way. It doesn't perpetuate itself. The moment we stop perpetuating it, it dies. Like everything else, it dies on its own. Meditation is not so much like doing something or going somewhere or acquiring this and that. Meditation is actually a way to stop feeding this unenlightened consciousness.

When we sit in silence, being in the present moment, what happens? Nothing happens. But sometimes there is a moment so liberating, so illuminating, that everything is gone. The self is gone. All of the story lines are gone and universal oneness is dancing in front of us.

In the realm of true meditation there is no such thing as a meditator or meditation. There is nothing to be done. The only thing that is happening is that we are no longer constructing illusions, so all illusions begin to wither away. Have you ever experienced that? Perhaps you have experienced that many times. The Buddhist master Shantideva compares that with a sudden strike of lightning in the dark of the night that illuminates the entire sky. In this metaphor the darkness is our old consciousness, permeated with habits and lifetimes of karmic tendencies. The lightning is the enlightenment experience.

This illustrates what happens in the realm of meditation because we have stopped pedaling the wheel of delusion, samsara. It means that ultimately we don't do anything, and that is a very difficult assignment. It turns out to be the most difficult assignment of all. It is much easier to do something because by doing something we can keep turning the wheel of delusion. Every time we decide that we like something or dislike something we are actually buying into the story line. We are feeding ego. We are perpetuating the wheel of delusion. Every time we compare ourselves with others that means that once again we are fueling the wheel of delusion. Every time we hold on to hatred and pride, we are once again perpetuating that. We are working very hard pushing that rolling ball of snow and making it heavier and thicker.

So meditation ultimately stops everything. We stop pushing that rolling snowball and we stop pedaling the bicycle. We don't do anything because there is nothing we can do. From that moment on we are no longer in charge. The truth is in charge. From that moment on truth is going to voluntarily destroy the foundation, the basis of all sorrow, all misery. Truth does that work for us. All we have to do is stop everything. That is what meditation is all about.

In the ancient times, spiritual seekers used various methods to practice meditation. Yet, there is only one meditation. That is a state of nondoing. When we stop trying to get somewhere and let go of all of our inner exertions, surprisingly the ineffable truth reveals itself to us. Then that's it. There is nothing else to be found. The realization of that truth sets us free from the prison of our imaginary self. When we go deeply into meditation, we always witness the dissolution of self. If the self is still sticking around, we have not gone deep enough. This is also true with prayer.

Prayer is not necessarily a religious act. The meaning behind prayer is surrendering the self. In Buddhism, prayer is not as important as it is in some other religions. Usually prayer is based on recognizing a duality between the self and the divine. It might be very shocking for some people to realize that in Buddhism the purpose of prayer is not about gaining something but about losing everything, including this beloved "I." Don't worry! There is nothing to lose except our false concepts. Eventually, even the idea of losing oneself dissolves too. There is nothing to be relinquished nothing to be gained.

Meditating is a little challenging in the beginning because it is challenging to pause everything. We have an egoic mind that is trained and habituated to do something, to construct this world of illusion. Ego is working very hard. Ego is always talking. Ego is making up stories for the sake of perpetuating all of the stories of the notion of "I." "I" am meditating. "I" am truly existent. "I" am truly meditating and now "I" am getting somewhere. "I" am chasing after enlightenment. This very thought is just ego's way of perpetuating itself. Sooner or later we are acutely aware of all of the mind games going on in our head and of all of our unconscious habits. Once all the mind's habits are gone, then, meditation will also disappear. When the illness is gone, we don't need any more medicine.

One Buddhist master said that the only way we can break down the mind's habits is to hold a meditation session 108 times every day for six months or something like that. How can we hold a meditation session 108 times every day? How do we do that? What the master is talking about is carrying meditation practice into everyday life when we are out in the world performing everyday duties. Actually, this is very similar to the art of pausing. We pause. The idea is that we pause 108 times. We just pause. We stop. We just stop perpetuating mind's habit and we rest in the present moment. We regain awareness. We regain awareness 108 times a day. If we can't do that 108 times a day, then we try twenty times a day; if we can't do that, then ten times a day or even less than that. One hundred eight times a day actually requires a lot of discipline but it would be worth a try. It is a method, a way of maintaining meditative awareness every day while we are in the ordinary world. If we are not in a monastery, then this is a way to be conscious in everyday life. This might be the only way that we can break the mind's habit.

Even to say "practice meditation" is a little tricky because remember that meditation is not to be practiced. Meditation is pausing. Somehow we have to use this language "practicing meditation" while remembering that actually it is not to be practiced. It is to pause in the natural state, just as it is. Totally pause. Once again we stop rolling that snowball.

When we look into our consciousness we find lots of old buddies. There's hatred: "Hey, it's good to see you again. Hello, pride, good to see you too. Fear, is this teaching going to overpower you? When is this meditation going to be over with? I am waiting for you. I am cooking some very delicious food. Relax, don't worry, I am waiting for you." Pride, guilt, and fear are our very old friends. They all go back to this one simple problem and that is clinging to this illusory, so-called self, "I." We are all carrying this imaginary self around day and night. We are trying to secure it at any cost. Sometimes, the spiritual path that we are on might be just another way to enforce it. Obviously, people have been using the notion of God or eternal life as a way to solidify this illusion. Eternal life in heaven somewhere means that this "I" never has to die.

The idea of surrender itself can be very beautiful. It is the direct doorway to the truth. It is the powerful act of dropping the self right away. People often have the tendency to surrender to something or someone outside of themselves. Surrendering to the guru is not true surrender, because then you become the surrenderer, which is another version of self. For that very reason Buddha discouraged people from surrendering to his personality. Of course we always surrender to his wisdom. The problem is that when we surrender to his personality we don't surrender to his wisdom. He told devotees not to take even his words on blind faith. He said we should question them before accepting them as truth.

Buddha never claimed to be a messiah. He was walking in a forest after his awakening and he ran into a group of bandits. They were so struck by his presence they asked him, "Who are you? Are you a god, an angel?" He said, "No." They asked, "Are you a holy man?" He said, "No." Then they asked him again, "Who are you?" He answered simply, "I am awake." He had just awakened from the dream of duality and the sleep of ignorance.

In the realm of true meditation, all of our unconscious habits are brought into the light of awareness, and we see clearly how insubstantial they are. We can let go of them sooner or later. Sometimes, there is the magical possibility of letting go of all of them right here, now. We simply let awareness shine inside of us. All inner darkness vanishes and our divine nature is revealed. As a matter of fact, our true nature has been waiting for us to be awakened to it from the very beginning.

Our true nature is like a beautiful, kind lover who wants to be with us. But we have turned down that invitation because of the fear of opening our heart. Even at this very moment our divine nature is inviting us to be one with it. To be one with it means to realize who we are.

If we are truly ready to witness this amazing union right now, we don't need to do anything. We don't have to go anywhere. We just stop all forms of searching. Then we'll witness that union right where we are. That is the highest meditation. It is called "meditation without meditation."

CHAPTER TWELVE

Transcendent Wisdom

The Highest Truth

B UDDHA WAS an ideal man for us. He cannot be put into any cat-
egory. He cannot be called either a believer or a nonbeliever. He
went beyond all man-made limitations. He was not even Buddhist in
the way that many people understand the term Buddhist. He transcended all of his identities. He realized boundless love within himself and he embodied the highest level of joy, which ultimately is the
only wealth there is. He taught a timeless wisdom and a universal path
that transcends all isms. We cannot realize his teaching as long as we
are either theistic or atheistic. His teaching was revealed from a nonconceptual source. That teaching is called Prajnaparamita and literally
it means "transcendent wisdom." It is not mere philosophy or religious
doctrine. It expresses the truth in the most direct way. It is the way to
realize the ultimate truth, the great emptiness.

In that sense Prajnaparamita is not knowledge to be learned. It is the
act of transcending everything in the moment, life and death, good and
bad, past and future. It is realization of the truth rather than speculation
about such freedom. It is not just a spiritual high which dissipates once

one's endorphins are exhausted. Some Buddhist traditions tend to stress the distinction between true realization and spiritual highs.

I heard a very funny story regarding this matter. One time a radical Buddhist teacher was talking about transcending one's attachment to life and death. One of his students, upon hearing this ultimate message, felt that he had already realized this transcendence. He went to meet with the teacher to report his accomplishment. The teacher was sitting by himself at the temple. The moment the student told the teacher that he had transcended life and death, to his surprise the teacher jumped up, grabbed him by the throat, and started choking him. After wrestling for a while, the student was able to throw the teacher to the ground and escape. He sat down outside the temple struggling to regain his breath. His neck was covered with dark bruises. Another student passed by and noticing the situation said with a smile, "Oh, I see that you have transcended life and death too." It seems that this was the radical method the master used to challenge his students' notions of authentic realization.

When realization happens you simply know that it is not just another spiritual high. A spiritual high is quite distinct from realization. We have to be careful about confusing one with the other. A spiritual high is like a rainbow that looks beautiful but has little lasting substance. Many people get spiritual highs at churches, ashrams, and temples. These experiences are enjoyable but they are not the highest truth. The truth must be realized because without it there is no liberation. Without it everything we do, everything we try is simply another way of wasting our precious time with meaningless speculation and futile effort.

But what is the highest truth? Who knows? Who has the key to open the golden box where the highest truth is hidden? Actually there are no words, there are no concepts, and there is no perfect language that encapsulates the highest truth. A spiritual high is ego's way to tempt us to settle for less. Of course we always have the choice to postpone the golden day of realization. There are numerous ways to postpone that golden opportunity. Ego is very good at that. Ego's main job is postponement and such postponement can sometimes be extremely entertaining, especially when we let ourselves get lost in our beautiful illusions.

When we come to the spiritual path we have to be very cautious. We have to be certain that we are not adding another illusion on top of the illusions we already have. When we look into our consciousness we see that we have many illusions. Everything is an illusion, especially this notion of "I." The story of my life is an illusion: my birth, my relationships, and so forth. They are all a story just like a movie. If something happens to my brain, much of this story will be immediately forgotten. Therefore in the ultimate sense it is not truly existent. It is illusion. We have to be careful when we come to the spiritual world so that we do not fall into the trap of accumulating new illusions. Believe it or not there are very beautiful illusions about the path, the journey, and the practices. Sometimes celebrating illusions can be very entertaining but the problem is that sooner or later illusions collapse. It's just a matter of time. When illusions collapse they collapse with a sense of disappointment, discouragement, and bitterness as well. Therefore this is actually the perfect time to stop repeating this old habit of glorifying, chasing, and holding on to illusion.

When one illusion doesn't work then we become disillusioned and we go around with our antennae up looking for another illusion. We look for one we don't associate with any memories of being disillusioned, one with no sense of disappointment. We look for something new, something different, something better. When we don't find an illusion we like, we make a big deal out of it. We say we're having a spiritual crisis. We're going through the dark night of the soul. We feel that the ground beneath our feet is shaky. We don't like being in darkness, in emptiness. We want to find an illusion that gives us comfort, that gives us what could be called a psychological massage. Soon we find another illusion, one that is full of promise.

When we get into a mood of complaining about life we often start telling this long epic, a story about our personal journey. It involves a series of misfortunes, trials, and tribulations. It often starts with being born into the wrong family, with the wrong parents, and with very inauspicious circumstances. This ego trip keeps on unfolding and unfolding. At the same time it is all illusion. Our egoic mind is simply producing these never-happened stories. Have you ever sat in front of someone who does nothing but complain? They talk about how miserable they are and about how hard they are trying. In the middle of listening to this sad story have you ever suddenly had the realization that actually they were just asleep, having a bad dream? None of what they were saying was actually real. We can turn this perspective toward ourselves and see that everything is illusion. It would be truly liberating to have that realization. That realization is very powerful. As long as we are following the path of Shakyamuni Buddha our discipline and our practice are all about dissolving. It is a beautiful path, a path of burning and destroying.

In human history many wars began with glorifying an illusion: illusions of perfection, illusions of creating a utopian society. This has been repeated over and over again in our history. Millions of people have died because of this tendency to glorify some illusion of perfection. We always have to be very mindful and ruthlessly intelligent so we don't add more illusions to the ones we already have. We already have enough illusions. We don't need new illusions. Of course we can buy newer, more sacred, holier illusions, but illusion is always illusion. It just keeps us from awakening.

Millions and millions of people have lost their lives in order to glorify some collective illusion such as ethnic purity or the creation of some kind of utopian world at any cost. Such illusions are based on ignorance. Countless wars have been fought between religions and sectarian strife continues to this day. No tradition can claim to be exempt. We not only defend our illusions, we are ready to attack anyone who challenges them.

Here in the West many people like Eastern illusions because they have already become disillusioned with American illusions. Now they are going around trying to buy Eastern illusions. These new illusions may work for a while because we don't have any heartache associated with them, no bad memories. But ultimately we must dissolve every illusion: American illusions, Eastern illusions, European illusions, and finally our own illusions. What is our main illusion? The illusion is that I am real. I am truly existent. This final illusion is the one we want to hold on to.

There are stages that we go through on the path of dissolution and sometimes the first stage is a bit painful. Sometimes it has a bitter taste because it is painful to lose what we are attached to. It's painful to lose anything at all. Did you ever experience going through your paperwork or your laundry and find that you have a lot of things that are worn out and totally useless? There are old bank statements, pictures, and tee shirts that are completely beyond wearing. They are useless, yet when we have to make the radical choice to throw them away it's painful because we have great memories attached to them. We wore that tee shirt when we fell in love or we wore that tee shirt when we won the lottery or we wore it the first time we went to some beautiful place. For these reasons dissolving illusions can sometimes be very painful.

When we look into our consciousness sometimes we see that there are countless illusions. As a matter of fact everything we believe to be reality is actually an illusion, believe it or not. When we hear this Prajnaparamita with an open heart, that truthful message that everything is illusory, sometimes it is painful. But that message has to be heard. Yet, the moment we worship a text or a set of knowledge about Prajnaparamita, it becomes dogma. Of course texts, theories, and other things can initiate realization in us if they are treated as simply the medium. They are not true Prajnaparamita. Just like a great Zen master once said: "Only 'no Zen' Zen is the real Zen." In the same way there is no real transcendent wisdom. Yet there is transcendent wisdom. It's painful. This might sound like one of those age-old paradoxical wisdom statements that can drive you crazy.

Dogma seems to be one of the biggest obstacles in many spiritual traditions. It is often disguised as the wisdom of an infallible lineage, while sometimes it is simply ego's creation for the purpose of postponing the true realization of oneness. As long as such spiritual teachings are based on dogma, they are dead wisdom, full of superstition. Not only will they not help us, they will bind us to more and more dualism. They only serve some weird and absurd authority. This might be why the famous Buddhist master Naropa had to run away from Nalanda, the most prestigious monastery of his time. He found a fisherman named Tilopa, who said that one cannot realize the truth simply through reading Buddhist scriptures, sutras and tantras.

What is transcendent wisdom? Let's inquire into that. Actually you can call it by many names, whatever name you prefer. It is a direct momentary process of dissolving all illusion right now, in this very moment. It is dissolving the illusion of pain, sorrow, and hatred. It is dissolving the illusion of self. There is a fire of awareness ignited in our consciousness which ruthlessly burns everything, without any exception. Sometimes it burns everything in a single moment and sometimes it burns one illusion after another. That burning process is transcendent wisdom. You can call it "transcendent wisdom" or you don't have to call it anything. It is really awareness, not conceptualization. It is momentary. It is direct experience. It is a realization of losing everything, losing all of our cherished ideas and concepts, sometimes even without any resistance. It is a beautiful way of losing everything, not a painful way.

It's good to lose everything sometimes. It is good to get out of the straitjacket and get free from everything that has been imprisoning us throughout many lifetimes. It is truly liberating to lose all of our cherished illusions, including the illusion of self. That is transcendent wisdom. We don't have to go anywhere, in the ultimate sense, to search for transcendent wisdom. The moment we begin to let all illusions fall apart then transcendent wisdom, or whatever name we use, begins to manifest in our consciousness. True transcendent wisdom is dissolution. True transcendent wisdom is that awareness.

What does this beautiful term "transcendent wisdom" really mean? It means transcending everything. Transcendent wisdom begs and demands that we dissolve or transcend everything. To realize transcendent wisdom means to dissolve all of our illusions, all of our concepts. It is called the mother of the buddhas. Why? This is because all of the buddhas of the past, present, and future become enlightened by realizing the true meaning of transcendent wisdom. Transcendent wisdom is simple because in the ordinary sense we don't have to do anything. That's the beauty of this path. We don't really have to do anything. However, sometimes the simplest thing can be the most difficult thing. Actually we have great difficulty not doing anything. Not doing anything doesn't mean just sitting around being sedentary like a happy vegetable. That is the wrong idea of doing nothing. Doing nothing means giving up all mental exertion, especially the mental exertion we use to sustain the illusion of "I," the illusory separation between self and other. When we give up this effort, then suddenly all illusions just go away. We really don't have to do anything. It's all about stopping. We simply stop perpetuating and holding on to illusions. The illusions don't have their own life force. They are ready to dissolve in each and every moment. It's just a matter of time. When we wholeheartedly decide to no longer sustain the illusions, they collapse.

If we close our eyes for a few moments and pay attention to our mind, we see that somebody is working very hard. Their main work, their full-time employment, is to come up with concepts, ideas, and story lines about the past, present, and future with one clear goal, sustaining this illusory reality. This full-time employee is called "ego." Its story line is "I'm good. I'm bad. I don't have enough money. Somebody hurt me and I must take revenge on that person. I don't have a soul mate. I'm too old. I'm too young," and so forth. All of these are concepts produced by ego. Trying to acquire enlightenment from the outside, from a very impressive teacher or from an exotic practice, is also an illusion. These are simply other ways ego uses to sustain its illusory reality.

However, when we decide wholeheartedly to no longer sustain illusions all of this collapses. It takes a lot of energy to keep producing these story lines to feed the nonexistent, illusory reality. Suddenly, when we stop producing concepts and ideas, when we stop feeding that illusory reality, when we stop associating with ego, it is very simple. It is simple to stop associating with ego. However, there are no twelve-step programs in transcendent wisdom. There is only the one-step program and that is to not associate with the ego. The moment we stop associating with ego it just immediately ceases right there. And in that moment we fall in love with the truth.

You have to be a little bit crazy to love the truth. It's a beautiful love. It's a true love when you love the truth but it really doesn't make sense to the rest of the mind. It is pretty challenging to open your heart and love the truth. There is no mental image that you can hold on to. It's neither existence nor nonexistence. It's beyond everything. It's beyond all labels. Therefore Buddha sometimes used this word "suchness" to describe this highest truth. To love the truth is to love suchness, to love what is. Suchness, or emptiness, goes beyond mental images and therefore you have to be a little bit or sometimes very crazy to love suchness. You have to be crazy to love emptiness because it is totally irrational according to ego's plan. It is totally irrational to love emptiness because it doesn't give us anything. Emptiness doesn't give us anything. It is just suchness. It is just what is.

The most beautiful love that we can experience is to be in love with truth because it is challenging. It is much easier to be in love with concepts, with mental images. Such love is the fire of Prajnaparamita. It can burn all of our concepts, beliefs, and isms. It takes everything away from our consciousness and leaves us nothing except what is eternal. This love is not emotional attachment like the love people have toward gurus. It is wisdom that sees the way things are. With that wisdom we are like a person walking with eyes wide open.

Once we embrace Prajnaparamita as our path we have no choice other than losing all of our illusions. It isn't painful to go through that process because we see that all we lose is all of our misery. We find inexpressible bliss within. Soon, our heart and mind are united in a realm of boundless compassion and fierce intelligence. We are able to live in the world just as we are, having much fun every day. We'll be as vast as the sky. Nothing will confine us. We aren't tied up in a straitjacket of all sorts of beliefs that prevent us from realizing the great truth, the realm of supreme perfection.

Glossary

Brahmin—One of the classes of ancient Indian society, traditionally priests and scholars.

Buddha Shakyamuni (563–483 BCE)—The founder of Buddhism. Born a prince of the Shakya clan, he left the palace to seek a way to the end of suffering. He became awakened, or enlightened, under a Bodhi tree. His path to awakening, Buddhism, the Middle Way, is beyond the extremes of self-indulgence and extreme asceticism.

Buddha Nature—The central concept in Buddhism that asserts that the true nature of each living being is already enlightened.

Dharma—This term has a number of meanings. Most commonly it is used to mean the teachings of the Buddha and the path to liberation that he taught.

Dukkha—Pain, suffering, sorrow, grief, unhappiness, that which is unsatisfactory; existential anguish, lack of peace.

Egoic Identity—Relating to a sense of individuality or separate self. States of consciousness confined to the limits of personal identity; these are relative, personal, and individual, the opposite of transpersonal.

Emptiness—The notion that all things are free from any fixed, independent, permanent existence. In Buddhist philosophy emptiness is synonymous with truth. Buddhism often describes truth as a state that goes beyond all intellectual comprehension.

Heart Sutra—The essence of the Buddhist teaching on Prajnaparamita, transcendent wisdom. It is recited daily in many communities all over the world.

Ju Mipham (1846–1912)—An eminent master of the Nyingma tradition and one of the greatest scholars of his time. His collected works fill more than thirty volumes.

Kabir (1398–1448)—A mystic, poet, and saint from northern India who was influenced by Hindu, Muslim, and Buddhist traditions but was not a follower of any specific tradition. His inspirational songs and poems embody deep wisdom and are loved by people all over the world.

Karma—The principle of cause and effect. It is also used to mean the result produced by past action.

Lama—The Tibetan word for teacher, spiritual advisor. *Guru* in Sanskrit.

Liberation—The recognition of one's identity with ultimate reality and a return to one's original state of perfection.

Machik Labdron (1055–1153)—The most famous Tibetan yogini, who initiated the meditation practice called Chod, or "cutting through."

Mantra—A sacred word or phrase of spiritual significance and power.

Mara—The "devil" that causes obstacles to spiritual practice and enlightenment.

Milarepa, Jetsun (1040–1123)—Tibet's great yogi and poet whose biography and poems are among the best-loved works in Tibetan Buddhism. He is the archetype of the perfect disciple, meditation practitioner, and teacher.

Nagarjuna (first–second centuries CE)—Indian master who composed numerous philosophical treatises expounding the doctrine of the Middle Way.

Nalanda University—From the fifth century CE until it was destroyed around 1200, one of the greatest Buddhist centers of learning in India.

Naropa (1016–1100)—An Indian pandita and siddha, the disciple of Tilopa, and the teacher of Marpa.

Nirvana—The enlightened state, beyond suffering.

Nyingma Tradition—The ancient or older tradition, which presents teachings propagated in Tibet by Padmasambhava in the eighth century.

Patrul Rinpoche (1808–1887)—A prolific writer and commentator from eastern Tibet, author of *Words of My Perfect Teacher*. A nonsectarian, he studied with all masters and is revered by all Tibetan Buddhist traditions. A wandering mendicant, a renunciant, he was known for his pure loving-kindness.

Prajnaparamita—The highest truth in Buddhism. It is a term for enlightened mind, free from all mental conditioning. Literally it means "transcendent wisdom." There are discourses called the *Prajnaparamita Sutras* that elucidate this theme.

Samsara—The cyclic existence of birth and death.

Shantideva (seventh century)—The great Indian poet and mahasiddha who astounded the monks of Nalanda with his famous poem on engaging in the practice of loving-kindness and the activities of a bodhisattva, called the *Bodhicharyavatara* (*The Way of the Bodhisattva*).

Siddha—A being that has attained high spiritual realization.

Sutra—A concise text containing the discourses of Shakyamuni Buddha or those inspired by him. Sutras are often in the format of a discourse between the Buddha and one of his followers.

Tantra—In Buddhism tantra is considered a transformative path involving skillful methodology. It is practiced in Tibet, Bhutan, Ladakh, and Nepal and is known as Vajrayana Buddhism.

Tilopa (988–1069)—One of the eighty-four mahasiddhas of India; teacher of Naropa.

Yogi and Yogini—Male and female practitioners of yoga or meditation; spiritual practitioners.

Dharmata Foundation carries the current inventory of Anam Thubten's books and recorded teachings on CD and DVD. For more information visit:

www.dharmatafoundation.org

Or mail:

Dharmata Foundation
235 Washington Avenue
Point Richmond, CA 94807

Anam Thubten travels nationally and internationally to lecture and teach. To obtain a schedule of Dharmata events email info@dharmata .org or call 510-233-7071.